Quiz-Quiz
Middle School Math
Level 2

Michael Smith

Kagan

Kagan Publishing
981 Calle Amanecer
San Clemente, CA 92673
1.800.933.2667
www.KaganOnline.com

ISBN: 978-1-933445-52-6

Quiz-Quiz-Trade

Table of Contents

Preface

Quiz-Quiz-Trade is an engaging, powerful structure for learning and reinforcing a wide variety of concepts in all grades and subject areas. Students are up, moving about, quizzing each other, coaching if necessary, praising each other, and learning embedded social skills.

Quiz-Quiz-Trade is a terrific review structure prior to a test. Students who would normally not ask clarification questions prior to a test can get their questions and misconceptions addressed in a safe environment among peers.

Quiz-Quiz-Trade can be used as a pre-assessment/ formative assessment tool as teachers can circulate Quiz-Quiz-Trade cards that cover the prerequisite skills that should already be in place in advance of an upcoming unit. Careful observation can help teachers decide if and what pre-teaching is necessary.

Quiz-Quiz-Trade also helps prevent memory loss over periods of time. For example, suppose a student learns about fractions at the beginning of the school year. The teacher in the succeeding year might not cover fractions until the latter part of the year. Consequently, the students will have gone over a year and a half since they last experienced fractions. Quiz-Quiz-Trade helps address that void by periodically refreshing student memory of concepts previously learned. The time required to review for midterms or other significant assessments is also minimized.

Some Quiz-Quiz-Trade cards can easily be used in reverse order. This works especially well for terms and definitions. Instruct students to show definitions first, so partners must identify the correct term. When you sense they are ready, instruct students to show the term first and have partners provide the definition of the term. This takes students to a higher level of thinking skill.

Printing advice: Print your Quiz-Quiz-Trade cards on cardstock and, if possible, laminate the cardstock before cutting out the cards. They will last much longer. Recipe cards are a durable alternative to cardstock.

There are a couple ways to differentiate Quiz-Quiz-Trade. First, you can print your cards on different colored cardstock with the intent that students will do Quiz-Quiz-Trade with students holding cards of the same color. Second, you can put three questions on each card. The first question can be challenging, the second can be grade appropriate, and the third question can be differentiated to help meet the needs of more students. When students begin Quiz-Quiz-Trade with a partner, they can choose the question that is appropriate for their ability level.

Quiz-Quiz-Trade cards can easily be adapted to use with other structures. If printed without the solutions or coaching tips on the back, they can be used for Fan-N-Pick, RallyQuiz, and Showdown.

About the Author

My teaching career began in August of 1984 following graduation from St. Thomas University with a bachelor of education degree. Most of my 30-plus years of teaching experience have been in mathematics from grades 6 to 12, with other teaching assignments in accounting, computer science, construction, economics, law, science, and social studies. I have been fortunate to have taught a variety of subjects at the middle and high school levels to students with a broad spectrum of abilities and needs. During this time, I have also worked as a school principal, numeracy lead, and professional development presenter.

I became interested in professional development in my first year of teaching as I was always looking for ways to improve my craft and meet the needs of all learners. I took advantage of several opportunities to attend various workshops relevant to teaching/learning and soon began delivering workshops myself.

My journey with Kagan Cooperative Learning began in May of 2006 when I attended a GLACIE conference in Toronto. Dr. Spencer Kagan delivered a full-day session on Brain-Friendly Teaching. This was a major turning point in my teaching career. First, the presentation style: Dr. Kagan shared a wealth of knowledge on Brain-Friendly Teaching in a passionate, convincing way. Participants were fully engaged throughout the day, and the structures presented were modeled and experienced. This was a dramatic change for me as I had endured "sit-and-get" presentations for over 20 years prior. Second, I quickly realized that "student engagement" was the missing ingredient in my personal quest to become a more effective classroom teacher and to better meet the needs of students—academic, social, and emotional.

In July of 2006, I attended the Kagan Summer Academy in Orlando. I was convinced this was to become my passion and focus for the rest of my career. The trainer, Tom Finegan, was very passionate, personable, professional, and engaging as a presenter. There wasn't one boring or dragging moment in the five-day training. This was the "wow moment" of my teaching career.

I eventually accumulated over 50 days of Kagan training by attending Kagan Structures Level II, Multiple Intelligences, Brain-Friendly Teaching, Cooperative Learning for Secondary Math, Cooperative Learning for Secondary Science, The Dynamic Trainer, Cooperative Meetings, Instructional Leadership Academy, and Kagan Win-Win Discipline.

My passion and enthusiasm for Kagan Cooperative Learning inspired me to become a Certified Kagan School Trainer for Kagan Publishing & Professional Development. I currently present Kagan Cooperative Learning Level I annually as a credit course through the New Brunswick Teachers' Association. The feedback is always very positive and encouraging.

In conclusion, Dr. Spencer Kagan, his wife Laurie, Miguel, and the entire team of Kagan trainers have created an absolute educational masterpiece that has the potential to totally restructure and reshape teaching and learning worldwide as we have known it.

Dedications & Appreciations

I would like to dedicate the efforts and intentions of this book to my wife Suzanne, daughters Jennifer and Kalie, and my parents David and Betty for their continued support and encouragement throughout my journey with Kagan Cooperative Learning and all the Kagan workshops I have attended since 2006.

I would like to extend my sincere appreciation to all former and current colleagues who have influenced me in the teaching profession in various ways and have genuinely expressed an interest in the learnings from the Kagan workshops I have attended.

A special thank you to the New Brunswick Teachers' Association for their moral and financial support to assist with costs associated with attending all the workshops since 2006.

I sincerely thank colleague and mathematics teacher Anthony Nolletti for assisting with the previewing and editing of my material prior to publication.

A special thank you to all the Kagan trainers with whom I have had the pleasure of learning from and sharing experiences with. You are all truly remarkable people and trainers!

Appreciation goes to Miguel Kagan for his guidance and review of my manuscript; Alex Core for making the book come alive with his design; Becky Herrington for managing the publication; Erin Kant for illustrations; Kirsten Zanze for proofreading; and Kim Fields for copy editing.

Quiz-Quiz-Trade

Students quiz a partner, get quizzed by a partner, and then trade cards to repeat the process with a new partner.

To play Quiz-Quiz-Trade, each student receives one card. The card has a question or problem on it. For example, a card in the Exploring Circles & Area set asks for the definition of a line bisector. With cards in hand, students stand up with a hand up and high five to pair up with a partner. Partner A uses the card to quiz the other partner. For example, Partner A asks Partner B, *"What is a line bisector?".* Partner B answers. If correct, Partner A offers praise: *"A line, ray, or segment which cuts another line segment into two equal parts is correct."* If incorrect, Partner A coaches. If it's a problem to solve, Partner A works it out, discussing it aloud. Next, partners switch roles and quiz the other way. After they have quizzed both ways, they trade cards and find a new partner to quiz, get quizzed, and trade again.

Quiz-Quiz-Trade is a great way to master content knowledge. It makes redundant quizzing an energizing, engaging event, contributing to a positive classroom climate. Quiz-Quiz-Trade is a student favorite as they love interacting with all their classmates.

Benefits

Students...

- ...repeatedly quiz each other.
- ...enjoy playing, thereby enhancing the class tone.
- ...interact with many classmates.
- ...make connections with partners.
- ...practice coaching each other.
- ...develop praising skills.

Kagan Publishing • 800.933.2667 • www.KaganOnline.com

Structure Power

Traditional worksheet drill and practice is boring. The same content taught with Quiz-Quiz-Trade becomes an exciting, energizing game! Students want to move, and they want to talk with each other. In the traditional classroom, we tell them, *"Sit down and don't talk."* We are going against students' basic impulses. And it turns out their impulses are right, and traditional worksheet work is wrong. When students move, they have more oxygen and glucose in the brain. And when they talk, their brains get more fully engaged. With Quiz-Quiz-Trade, students move and talk, but we channel that energy into learning. It is win-win. Students get to do what they most want while we get what we most want—student learning!

Tips

- **Unfold the Answer.** The quiz cards in this book are designed to be folded, so the question is on one side, and the answer is on the other. When students pair up to quiz, they show their partner the quiz question only. The answer is folded back. When it is time to show the answer, the answer is unfolded so that students can see the question and answer at the same time. Seeing the question and answer at the same time often aids in remembering the content.

Differentiated Instruction

Two different sets of question cards may be made, differentiated by content or difficulty. The cards are color-coded, and students are instructed to pair up with others who have the same color.

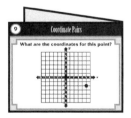 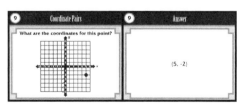

- **Tips on Cards.** The quiz cards can have two tips. If a student answers incorrectly or asks for a tip, the quizzing student provides a tip from the card.

- **Student Cards.** Have students make their own quiz cards. The cards have the question on the front and the answer on the back (3" x 5" index cards work well). Have students submit the cards first for the teacher to review for accuracy.

How to Play
Quiz-Quiz-Trade

Students quiz a partner, get quizzed by a partner, and then trade cards to repeat the process with a new partner.

1

Students Pair Up:

With a card in one hand and the other hand raised, each student stands up, puts a hand up, and pairs up with a classmate. They give each other a high five as they pair up.

2

Partner A Quizzes:

In the pair, Partner A asks Partner B the question on his or her card. For example, *"What is the difference between an equation and an expression?"*

3

Partner B Answers:

Partner B answers Partner A's question. *"An equation is a mathematical statement that two expressions are equal. An expression contains numbers and/or variables but is not equated to anything."*

Partner A Praises or Coaches:

Partner A opens the card to display the correct answer. If Partner B answered correctly, Partner A praises him or her. *"Excellent work!"* If Partner B answered incorrectly, Partner A coaches or tutors Partner B.

Switch Roles:

Partners switch roles. Partner B now asks the question on his or her card and offers praise or coaches.

Partners Trade Cards:

Before departing and looking for new partners, partners trade cards. This way, students have a new card for each new pairing.

Partners Continue Quizzing and Trading:

Partners split up and continue quizzing and getting quizzed by new partners. When done, they trade cards again and find a new partner.

Problems to Solve

Some of the card sets in this book require students to work out the answers. Here are a few tips to make problem-solving more effective in pairs.

1. **Dry-Erase Boards.** In addition to a quiz card, each student is given a dry-erase board and a marker. To solve the problem, they take a knee or sit down, and work out the problem on their board. Clipboards with a scratch sheet of paper are another way to have students work out problems as they circulate throughout the classroom.

2. **Side-by-Side.** Partners sit, kneel, or stand side-by-side so that they can see each other's work as they solve the problems.

3. **Talk It Out.** While solving problems, students talk aloud about their thinking. This helps partners hear how to solve the problem and allows the coaching partner to spot any mistakes.

What's in This Book?

This book contains 16 sets of cards that quiz on various mathematics skills. Each card set contains 32 quiz cards. These cards work well for partner work or with the whole class.

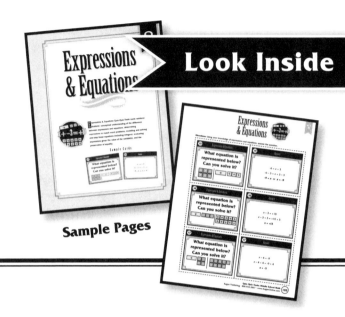

Look Inside

Sample Pages

How to Use Card Sets

• Copy each card set page and card set label.

• Cut along the guidelines.

• Fold each card so that there are two sides, a question side and an answer side.

• Laminate if possible. Another option is to print on cardstock.

Playing Tips

• **Coaching Tips.** If one partner answers incorrectly or asks for a tip, it is the other partner's job to coach. Here are two effective coaching strategies students can use with Quiz-Quiz-Trade:

1. Tip, Tip, Teach, Try Again. The coach provides one tip, and then asks the question again. If still incorrect, the coach provides a second tip and then reasks the question. If still incorrect, the coach instructs and then reasks the question. The coach praises his or her partner when the partner answers correctly.

2. Tell and Teach. The coach provides the answer and teaches his or her partner how to reach or remember the answer.

• **Model It.** Before playing for the first time, the teacher selects a student and models the Quiz-Quiz-Trade process for the class.

• **Hand Up.** Be sure to enforce the Hand Up Rule: students put up one hand while looking for a partner. This makes it quick and easy for students to tell who needs a partner. Students give a high five to pair up, then lower their hands.

• **Move Out.** For management, you may have students move to the center of the room when looking for a partner, and have pairs move out from the center of the room while quizzing each other.

• **Take a Knee.** Some teachers like to have students take a knee when they find a partner to quiz (kneel down on one knee). Standing students are still looking for a partner.

Card Labels

Each card set has a card label that goes in front of the set to help identify the cards. Use them to help identify sets when storing them or as an opener if you put them on a ring. ▶

Expressions & Equations

$$x + {}^-3 = {}^+10$$

Storage Tips

Put away each card set separately:
- Paper clip/binder clip the set together.
- Hole-punch a corner of each card and put them all on a ring.
- Place each card set in separate resealable, plastic sandwich bags or catalog envelopes.

Store games together:
- Keep all the same games together, and label the class set, so they are ready for next time!

Storage

More Kagan Structures

(alternatives to Quiz-Quiz-Trade for the Quiz-Quiz-Trade cards)

Here are three more structures you can use with the card sets in this book.

Fan-N-Pick

Students sit in teams of four. Student #1 holds the cards in his or her hand in a fan. Student #1 says to Student #2, *"Pick a card, any card."* Student #2 picks a card and reads the question aloud to the team. Student #3 is responsible for answering. Student #4 responds to the answer. If the answer is correct, Student #4 offers a praiser. If incorrect, Student #4 coaches or leads the team in coaching. The cards are passed one student to the left, and every role is rotated clockwise, too. So the student who picked and read a card now fans the cards. The student to his or her left now picks and reads a card, and so on.

RallyQuiz

Students sit in pairs. Each pair receives the set of cards. They place the pile of cards between them, question side up. Partner A selects the top card, displays the question, and reads it aloud to Partner B. Partner B responds. Partner A displays the answer. If Partner B was correct, Partner A offers a praiser like, *"Sweet!"* If the answer was incorrect, Partner A coaches. Next, Partner B selects the next card to quiz Partner A. They alternate quizzing each other with each new question card.

Showdown

Students sit in teams of four. Each teammate has a dry-erase board and a marker. The card set is placed in the center of the team with the question side facing up. Student #1 is the Showdown Captain. The Captain selects a card, reads it aloud to the team, and places it face up so that everyone can see the question. The Captain instructs everyone to quickly write their answer on their board and put their markers down when done. When everyone has an answer, the Showdown Captain says, *"Showdown!"* Everyone on the team shows their answer. If they all have the correct answer, they do a team celebration like a team high five. If one or more teammates have it incorrect, they explain why the correct answer is correct and how best to remember it. The Showdown Captain role is rotated for each new question.

Algebraic Expressions

Algebraic Expressions Quiz-Quiz-Trade cards reinforce students' conceptual understanding of creating a mathematical expression to match written words. For example, four more than a number would be expressed as $n + 4$.

Sample Cards

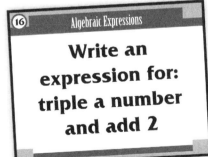

16   Algebraic Expressions

Write an expression for: triple a number and add 2

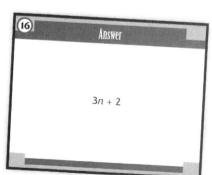

16   Answer

$3n + 2$

Algebraic Expressions

Directions: Create a mathematical expression representing the written words.

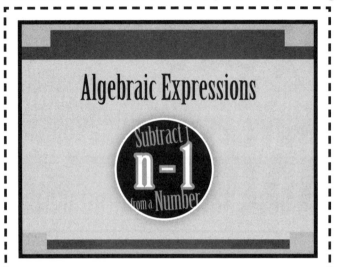

Algebraic Expressions

Subtract 1
n-1
from a Number

Card Set Label

When it's time to store this set, place this card label at the top of the set so that it's easy to identify for the next use.

① Algebraic Expressions
Write an expression for: 2 more than a number

① Answer
$n + 2$

② Algebraic Expressions
Write an expression for: a number multiplied by 3

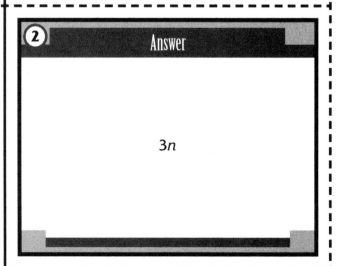

② Answer
$3n$

Quiz-Quiz-Trade: Middle School Math
Kagan Publishing · 800.933.2667 · www.KaganOnline.com

Algebraic Expressions

Directions: Create a mathematical expression representing the written words.

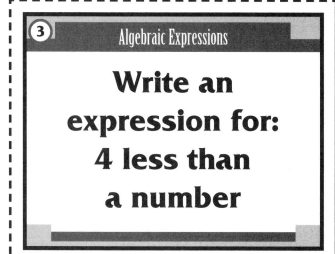

3 Algebraic Expressions

Write an expression for: 4 less than a number

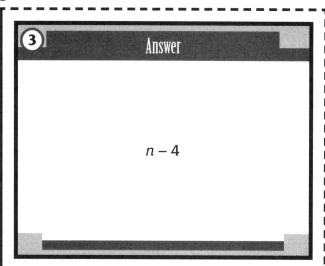

3 Answer

$n - 4$

4 Algebraic Expressions

Write an expression for: a number divided by 5

4 Answer

$\dfrac{n}{5}$

5 Algebraic Expressions

Write an expression for: a number increased by 6

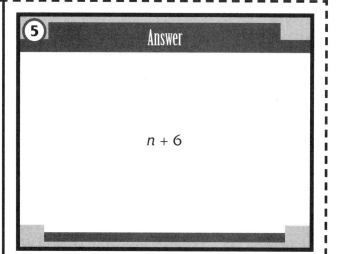

5 Answer

$n + 6$

Subtract 1
n – 1
from a Number

Algebraic Expressions

Directions: Create a mathematical expression representing the written words.

6 Algebraic Expressions

Write an expression for: a number decreased by 7

6 Answer

$$n - 7$$

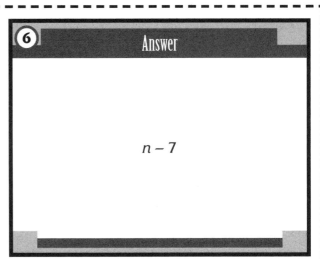

7 Algebraic Expressions

Write an expression for: double a number and add 8

7 Answer

$$2n + 8$$

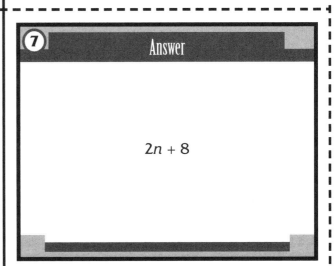

8 Algebraic Expressions

Write an expression for: a number is subtracted from 9

8 Answer

$$9 - n$$

Algebraic Expressions

Directions: Create a mathematical expression representing the written words.

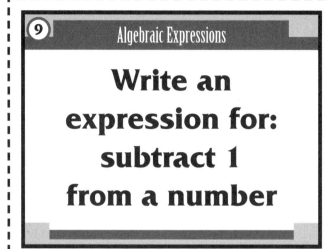

9 Algebraic Expressions

Write an expression for: subtract 1 from a number

9 Answer

$$n - 1$$

10 Algebraic Expressions

Write an expression for: 5 more than a number

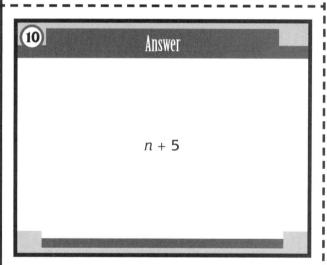

10 Answer

$$n + 5$$

11 Algebraic Expressions

Write an expression for: a number multiplied by 6

11 Answer

$$6n$$

Algebraic Expressions

Directions: Create a mathematical expression representing the written words.

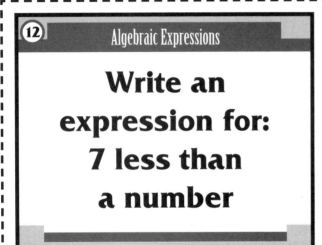

12 Algebraic Expressions

Write an expression for: 7 less than a number

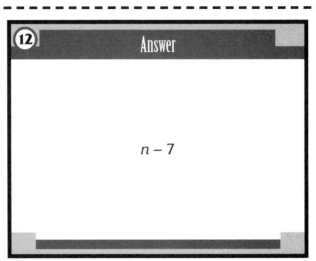

12 Answer

$$n - 7$$

13 Algebraic Expressions

Write an expression for: a number divided by 8

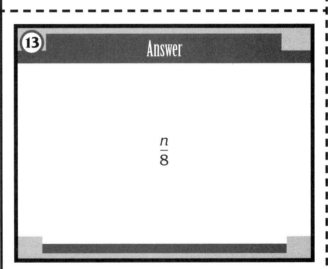

13 Answer

$$\frac{n}{8}$$

14 Algebraic Expressions

Write an expression for: a number increased by 9

14 Answer

$$n + 9$$

Algebraic Expressions

Directions: Create a mathematical expression representing the written words.

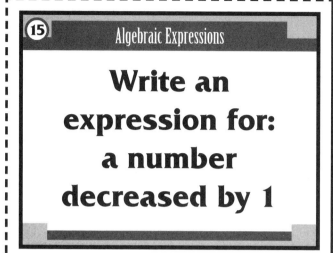

15 Algebraic Expressions

Write an expression for: a number decreased by 1

15 Answer

$n - 1$

16 Algebraic Expressions

Write an expression for: triple a number and add 2

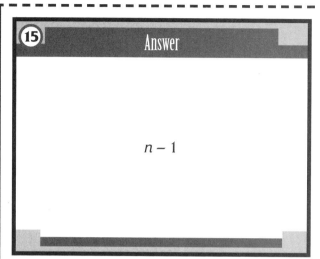

16 Answer

$3n + 2$

17 Algebraic Expressions

Write an expression for: a number is subtracted from 3

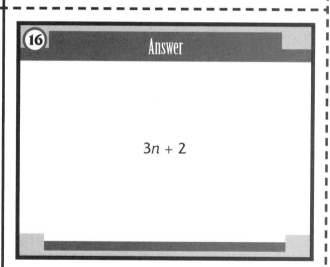

17 Answer

$3 - n$

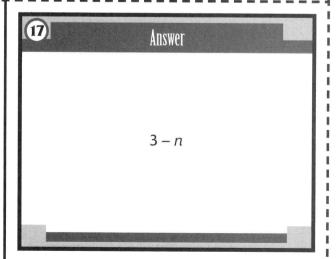

Algebraic Expressions

Directions: Create a mathematical expression representing the written words.

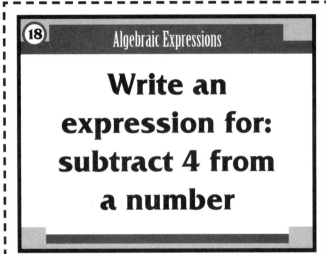

18 Algebraic Expressions

Write an expression for: subtract 4 from a number

18 Answer

$$n - 4$$

19 Algebraic Expressions

Write an expression for: 8 more than a number

19 Answer

$$n + 8$$

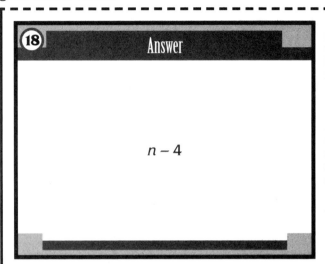

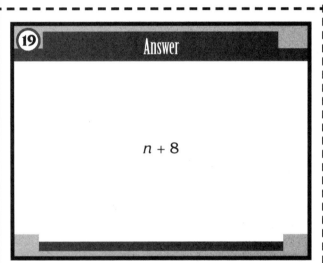

20 Algebraic Expressions

Write an expression for: a number multiplied by 9

20 Answer

$$9n$$

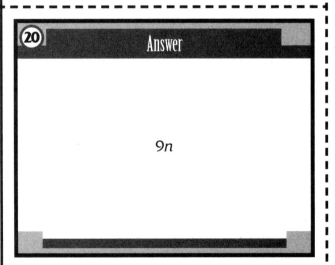

Algebraic Expressions

Directions: Create a mathematical expression representing the written words.

21 Algebraic Expressions

Write an expression for: 1 less than a number

21 Answer

$n - 1$

22 Algebraic Expressions

Write an expression for: a number divided by 2

22 Answer

$\dfrac{n}{2}$

23 Algebraic Expressions

Write an expression for: a number increased by 3

23 Answer

$n + 3$

Algebraic Expressions

Directions: Create a mathematical expression representing the written words.

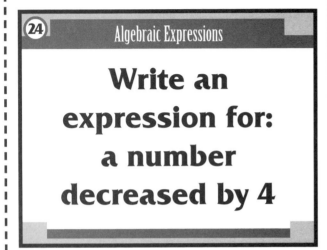

24 Algebraic Expressions

Write an expression for: a number decreased by 4

24 Answer

$n - 4$

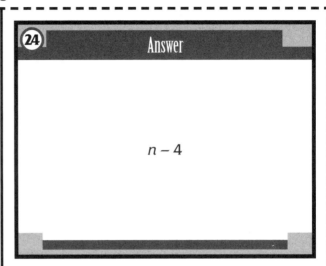

25 Algebraic Expressions

Write an expression for: quadruple a number and add 5

25 Answer

$4n + 5$

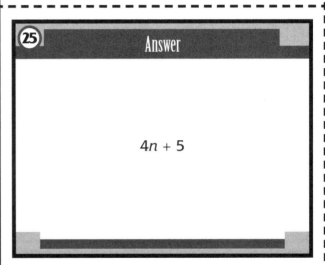

26 Algebraic Expressions

Write an expression for: a number is subtracted from 6

26 Answer

$6 - n$

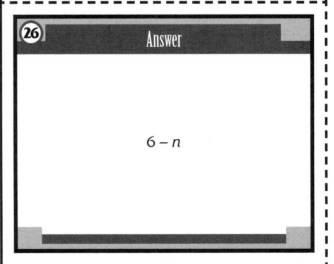

Algebraic Expressions

Directions: Create a mathematical expression representing the written words.

27 Algebraic Expressions **Write an expression for: subtract 7 from a number**	**27** Answer $n - 7$
28 Algebraic Expressions **Write an expression for: 3 more than twice a number**	**28** Answer $2n + 3$
29 Algebraic Expressions **Write an expression for: a number tripled and increased by 4**	**29** Answer $3n + 4$

Algebraic Expressions

Directions: Create a mathematical expression representing the written words.

---

(30) Algebraic Expressions

Write an expression for: a number doubled and increased by 1

(30) Answer

$2n + 1$

---

(31) Algebraic Expressions

Write an expression for: a number tripled and decreased by 5

(31) Answer

$3n - 5$

---

(32) Algebraic Expressions

Write an expression for: a number doubled and reduced by 3

(32) Answer

$2n - 3$

All About Fractions

All About Fractions Quiz-Quiz-Trade cards reinforce students' conceptual understanding of the relationship among fractions and decimals, repeating and terminating decimals, modeling the addition and subtraction of fractions pictorially, and adding and subtracting fractions symbolically.

Sample Cards

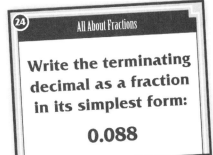

24 **All About Fractions**

Write the terminating decimal as a fraction in its simplest form:

0.088

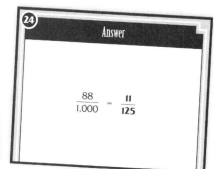

24 **Answer**

$$\frac{88}{1,000} = \frac{11}{125}$$

All About Fractions

Directions: Answer the question using your knowledge of fractions.

All About Fractions

Card Set Label

When it's time to store this set, place this card label at the top of the set so that it's easy to identify for the next use.

---

1 All About Fractions

What is a fraction in simplest form?

---

1 Answer

A fraction in simplest form is a fraction with a numerator and denominator that have no common factors, other than 1.

Example: $\frac{3}{5}$

---

2 All About Fractions

What are related denominators?

---

2 Answer

Related denominators are two fractions where the denominator of one fraction is a factor of the other.

Examples:

$\frac{1}{5}$ and $\frac{3}{5}$ or $\frac{1}{4}$ and $\frac{5}{12}$

All About Fractions

Directions: Answer the question using your knowledge of fractions.

---

3 — All About Fractions

Define unrelated denominators.

3 — Answer

Unrelated denominators are two fractions where the denominators have no common factor of the other.

Examples:

$\frac{1}{5}$ and $\frac{3}{7}$ or $\frac{1}{3}$ and $\frac{7}{8}$

---

4 — All About Fractions

Define common denominator.

4 — Answer

A common denominator is a number that is a common factor for each of the given numbers.

Examples:

$\frac{1}{3}$ and $\frac{3}{4}$ and $\frac{7}{12}$

---

5 — All About Fractions

What is a unit fraction?

5 — Answer

A unit fraction is a fraction that has a numerator of 1.

Examples:

$\frac{1}{2}$ or $\frac{1}{5}$

All About Fractions

Directions: Answer the question using your knowledge of fractions.

6 — All About Fractions

If $\frac{1}{8} = 0.125$, what is $\frac{3}{8}$ as a decimal?

6 — Answer

0.375

3×0.125

7 — All About Fractions

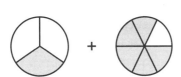

Express as an improper fraction and as a mixed number.

7 — Answer

$$\frac{1}{3} + \frac{5}{6} = \frac{2}{6} + \frac{5}{6} = \frac{7}{6}$$

$$\frac{7}{6} = 1\frac{1}{6}$$

8 — All About Fractions

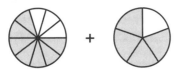

Express as an improper fraction and as a mixed number.

8 — Answer

$$\frac{7}{10} + \frac{4}{5} = \frac{7}{10} + \frac{8}{10} = \frac{15}{10}$$

$$\frac{15}{10} = 1\frac{5}{10} = 1\frac{1}{2}$$

All About Fractions

Directions: Answer the question using your knowledge of fractions.

---

9 All About Fractions

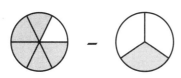

Express as an improper fraction and as a mixed number.

---

9 Answer

$$\frac{3}{4} + \frac{7}{8} = \frac{6}{8} + \frac{7}{8} = \frac{13}{8}$$

$$\frac{13}{8} = 1\frac{5}{8}$$

---

10 All About Fractions

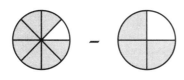

What does this model? What is the answer?

---

10 Answer

$$\frac{5}{6} - \frac{1}{3}$$

$$\frac{5}{6} - \frac{2}{6} = \frac{3}{6} = \frac{1}{2}$$

---

11 All About Fractions

What does this model? What is the answer?

---

11 Answer

$$\frac{7}{8} - \frac{3}{4}$$

$$\frac{7}{8} - \frac{6}{8} = \frac{1}{8}$$

All About Fractions

Directions: Answer the question using your knowledge of fractions.

12 All About Fractions

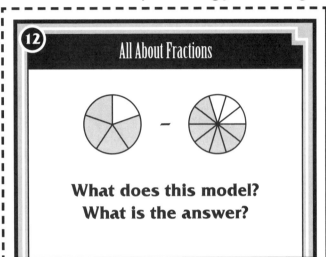

What does this model?
What is the answer?

12 Answer

$$\frac{4}{5} - \frac{7}{10}$$

$$\frac{8}{10} - \frac{7}{10} = \frac{1}{10}$$

13 All About Fractions

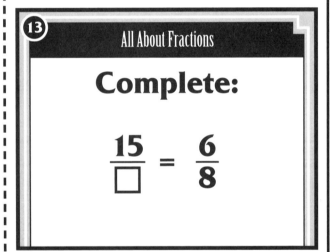

Complete:

$$\frac{15}{\square} = \frac{6}{8}$$

13 Answer

$6 \times 2.5 = 15$

So $8 \times 2.5 = 20$

$$\frac{15}{20} = \frac{6}{8}$$

14 All About Fractions

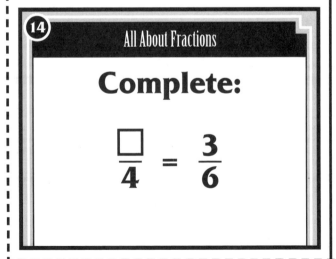

Complete:

$$\frac{\square}{4} = \frac{3}{6}$$

14 Answer

$6 \div 2 = 3$

So $4 \div 2 = 2$

$$\frac{2}{4} = \frac{3}{6}$$

All About Fractions

Directions: Answer the question using your knowledge of fractions.

---

15 All About Fractions

Complete:

$$\frac{3}{4} = \frac{6}{\square}$$

---

15 Answer

$3 \times 2 = 6$

So $4 \times 2 = 8$

$$\frac{3}{4} = \frac{6}{8}$$

---

16 All About Fractions

Write this mixed number as an improper fraction:

$$3\frac{2}{3}$$

---

16 Answer

$3 \times 3 + 2 = 11$

$$\frac{11}{3}$$

---

17 All About Fractions

Write this mixed number as an improper fraction:

$$2\frac{2}{5}$$

---

17 Answer

$2 \times 5 + 2 = 12$

$$\frac{12}{5}$$

All About Fractions

Directions: Answer the question using your knowledge of fractions.

---

18 | All About Fractions

Write this mixed number as an improper fraction:

$$1\frac{3}{4}$$

---

18 | Answer

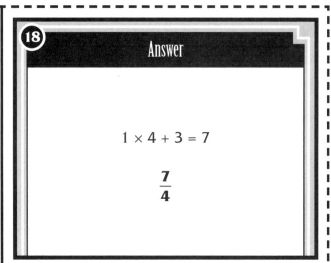

$$1 \times 4 + 3 = 7$$

$$\frac{7}{4}$$

---

19 | All About Fractions

Write this mixed number as an improper fraction:

$$\frac{15}{4}$$

---

19 | Answer

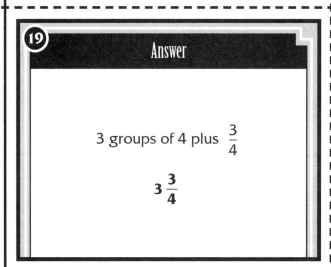

3 groups of 4 plus $\frac{3}{4}$

$$3\frac{3}{4}$$

---

20 | All About Fractions

Write this improper fraction as a mixed number:

$$\frac{7}{3}$$

---

20 | Answer

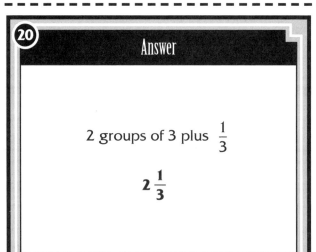

2 groups of 3 plus $\frac{1}{3}$

$$2\frac{1}{3}$$

Directions: Answer the question using your knowledge of fractions.

---

21   All About Fractions

Write this improper fraction as a mixed number:

$$\dfrac{9}{2}$$

---

21   Answer

4 groups of 2 plus $\dfrac{1}{2}$

$4\dfrac{1}{2}$

---

22   All About Fractions

Write the terminating decimal as a fraction in its simplest form:

0.8

---

22   Answer

$$\dfrac{8}{10} = \dfrac{4}{5}$$

---

23   All About Fractions

Write the terminating decimal as a fraction in its simplest form:

0.08

---

23   Answer

$$\dfrac{8}{100} = \dfrac{2}{25}$$

All About Fractions

Directions: Answer the question using your knowledge of fractions.

---

24 All About Fractions

Write the terminating decimal as a fraction in its simplest form:

0.088

---

24 Answer

$$\frac{88}{1,000} = \frac{11}{125}$$

---

25 All About Fractions

Write the repeating decimal as a fraction in its simplest form:

$0.\overline{3}$

---

25 Answer

$$\frac{33}{99} = \frac{3}{9} = \frac{1}{3}$$

---

26 All About Fractions

Write the repeating decimal as a fraction in its simplest form:

$0.\overline{02}$

---

26 Answer

$$\frac{2}{99}$$

Quiz-Quiz-Trade: Middle School Math
Kagan Publishing · 800.933.2667 · www.KaganOnline.com

All About Fractions

Directions: Answer the question using your knowledge of fractions.

---

27 | All About Fractions

Write the repeating decimal as a fraction in its simplest form:

$0.\overline{43}$

27 | Answer

$\dfrac{43}{99}$

---

28 | All About Fractions

Write the following fraction as a decimal number:

$\dfrac{11}{50}$

28 | Answer

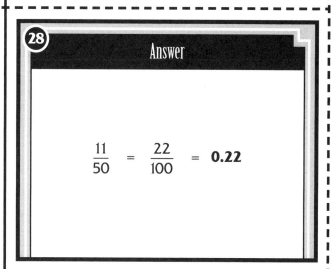

$\dfrac{11}{50} = \dfrac{22}{100} = \textbf{0.22}$

---

29 | All About Fractions

Write the following fraction as a decimal number:

$\dfrac{17}{25}$

29 | Answer

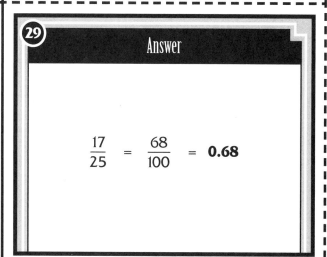

$\dfrac{17}{25} = \dfrac{68}{100} = \textbf{0.68}$

All About Fractions

Directions: Answer the question using your knowledge of fractions.

(30) All About Fractions

Write the following fraction as a decimal number:

$$\frac{13}{20}$$

(30) Answer

$$\frac{13}{20} \;=\; \frac{65}{100} \;=\; 0.65$$

(31) All About Fractions

Solve:

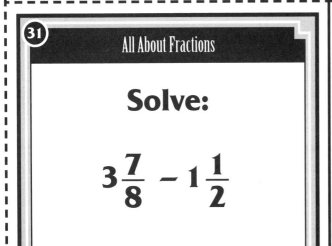

$$3\frac{7}{8} - 1\frac{1}{2}$$

(31) Answer

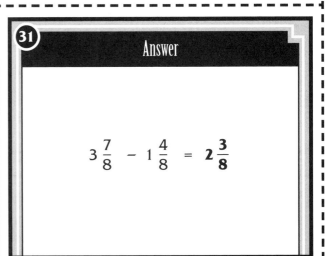

$$3\frac{7}{8} - 1\frac{4}{8} = 2\frac{3}{8}$$

(32) All About Fractions

Solve:

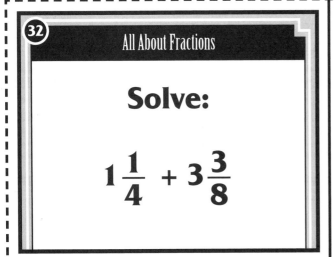

$$1\frac{1}{4} + 3\frac{3}{8}$$

(32) Answer

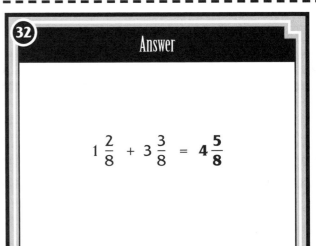

$$1\frac{2}{8} + 3\frac{3}{8} = 4\frac{5}{8}$$

Comparing & Ordering Fractions, Decimals & Percents

Comparing & Ordering Fractions, Decimals & Percents Quiz-Quiz-Trade cards reinforce students' conceptual understanding of how fractions, decimals, and percent relate to each other; how to convert among them; and how to order them from least to greatest and vice versa.

Sample Cards

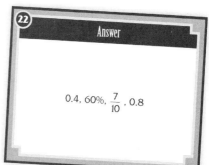

22 Comparing & Ordering Fractions, Decimals & Percents

Order the following from smallest to largest:

$0.8,\ \dfrac{7}{10},\ 0.4,\ 60\%$

22 Answer

$0.4,\ 60\%,\ \dfrac{7}{10},\ 0.8$

Comparing & Ordering Fractions, Decimals & Percents

Directions: Solve the problem using your knowledge of fractions, decimals, and percents.

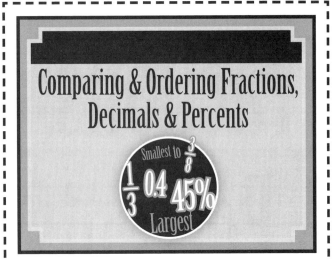

Comparing & Ordering Fractions, Decimals & Percents

Smallest to $\frac{3}{8}$

$\frac{1}{3}$ 0.4 45%

Largest

Card Set Label

When it's time to store this set, place this card label at the top of the set so that it's easy to identify for the next use.

---

1 Comparing & Ordering Fractions, Decimals & Percents

Define terminating decimal.

1 Answer

A terminating decimal is a mathematical expression representing the division of one whole number by another. The result is a finite number.

Example: $\frac{1}{8}$ = 0.125

---

2 Comparing & Ordering Fractions, Decimals & Percents

Define repeating decimal.

2 Answer

A repeating decimal is a decimal with a repeating pattern in the digits that follow the decimal point. It is written with a bar above the repeating digits.

Example: $\frac{1}{12}$ = 0.08333 = 0.08$\overline{3}$

Comparing & Ordering Fractions, Decimals & Percents

Directions: Solve the problem using your knowledge of fractions, decimals, and percents.

---

3 Comparing & Ordering Fractions, Decimals & Percents

What is a fraction?

---

3 Answer

A fraction is a number between zero and 1 and is expressed as one number (numerator) over another number (denominator).

Example: $\frac{2}{3}$

---

4 Comparing & Ordering Fractions, Decimals & Percents

What is a percent?

---

4 Answer

A percent is the number of parts per 100: the numerator of a fraction with a denominator of 100.

Example: $\frac{3}{4} = \frac{75}{100} = 75\%$

---

5 Comparing & Ordering Fractions, Decimals & Percents

Is $\frac{7}{16}$ closer to 0, $\frac{1}{2}$, or 1?

---

5 Answer

$\frac{8}{16}$ is equal to $\frac{1}{2}$

so $\frac{7}{16}$ is closer to $\frac{1}{2}$

Comparing & Ordering Fractions, Decimals & Percents

Directions: Solve the problem using your knowledge of fractions, decimals, and percents.

6 Comparing & Ordering Fractions, Decimals & Percents

How are decimals, fractions, and percents alike?

6 Answer

Decimals, fractions, and percents are all different ways of expressing a part of a whole.

7 Comparing & Ordering Fractions, Decimals & Percents

What is $\frac{1}{4}$ as a decimal? A percent?

7 Answer

0.25 and 25%

8 Comparing & Ordering Fractions, Decimals & Percents

What is $\frac{7}{10}$ as a decimal? A percent?

8 Answer

0.7 and 70%

Comparing & Ordering Fractions, Decimals & Percents

Directions: Solve the problem using your knowledge of fractions, decimals, and percents.

9 Comparing & Ordering Fractions, Decimals & Percents

What is $\frac{1}{3}$ as a decimal? A percent?

9 Answer

$0.\overline{3}$ and 33%

10 Comparing & Ordering Fractions, Decimals & Percents

What is $\frac{4}{5}$ as a decimal? A percent?

10 Answer

0.8 and 80%

11 Comparing & Ordering Fractions, Decimals & Percents

What is $\frac{3}{4}$ as a decimal? A percent?

11 Answer

0.75 and 75%

Comparing & Ordering Fractions, Decimals & Percents

Directions: Solve the problem using your knowledge of fractions, decimals, and percents.

12 Comparing & Ordering Fractions, Decimals & Percents

What is $\frac{2}{5}$ as a decimal? A percent?

12 Answer

0.4 and 40%

13 Comparing & Ordering Fractions, Decimals & Percents

Is $\frac{5}{8}$ a terminating or repeating decimal?

13 Answer

terminating

0.625

14 Comparing & Ordering Fractions, Decimals & Percents

Is $\frac{5}{6}$ a terminating or repeating decimal?

14 Answer

repeating

$0.8\overline{3}$

Comparing & Ordering Fractions, Decimals & Percents

Directions: Solve the problem using your knowledge of fractions, decimals, and percents.

15 Comparing & Ordering Fractions, Decimals & Percents

What does one hundredth look like as a fraction? A decimal?

15 Answer

$\frac{1}{100}$ and 0.01

16 Comparing & Ordering Fractions, Decimals & Percents

What is the decimal equivalent of $\frac{56}{100}$?

16 Answer

0.56

17 Comparing & Ordering Fractions, Decimals & Percents

What is the decimal equivalent of $\frac{3}{5}$?

17 Answer

0.6

Comparing & Ordering
Fractions, Decimals & Percents

Directions: Solve the problem using your knowledge of fractions, decimals, and percents.

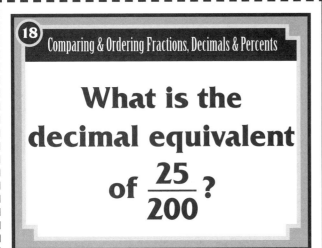

18 Comparing & Ordering Fractions, Decimals & Percents

What is the decimal equivalent of $\frac{25}{200}$?

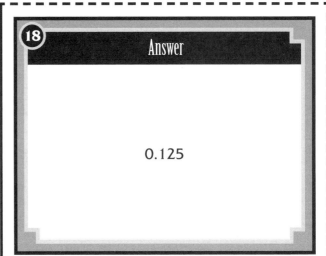

18 Answer

0.125

19 Comparing & Ordering Fractions, Decimals & Percents

What is the decimal equivalent of $\frac{7}{100}$?

19 Answer

0.07

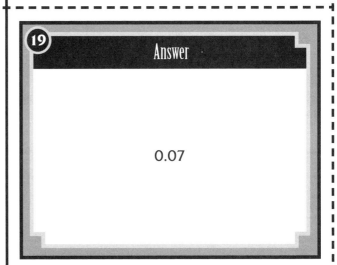

20 Comparing & Ordering Fractions, Decimals & Percents

What is the decimal equivalent of $\frac{625}{1,000}$?

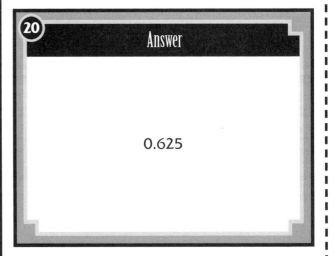

20 Answer

0.625

Comparing & Ordering Fractions, Decimals & Percents

Directions: Solve the problem using your knowledge of fractions, decimals, and percents.

---

21 Comparing & Ordering Fractions, Decimals & Percents

Order the following from smallest to largest:

$$35\%, \quad \frac{7}{10}, \quad 0.139, \quad \frac{9}{100}$$

---

21 Answer

$$\frac{9}{100}, \ 0.139, \ 35\%, \ \frac{7}{10}$$

---

22 Comparing & Ordering Fractions, Decimals & Percents

Order the following from smallest to largest:

$$0.8, \quad \frac{7}{10}, \quad 0.4, \quad 60\%$$

---

22 Answer

$$0.4, \ 60\%, \ \frac{7}{10}, \ 0.8$$

---

23 Comparing & Ordering Fractions, Decimals & Percents

Order the following from smallest to largest:

$$\frac{3}{8}, \quad 0.4, \quad \frac{1}{3}, \quad 45\%$$

---

23 Answer

$$\frac{1}{3}, \ \frac{3}{8}, \ 0.4, \ 45\%$$

Comparing & Ordering Fractions, Decimals & Percents

Directions: Solve the problem using your knowledge of fractions, decimals, and percents.

---

24 Comparing & Ordering Fractions, Decimals & Percents

Order the following from largest to smallest:

$$0.65, \frac{3}{5}, 0.8, 75\%$$

24 Answer

$$0.8, 75\%, 0.65, \frac{3}{5}$$

---

25 Comparing & Ordering Fractions, Decimals & Percents

Order the following from largest to smallest:

$$55\%, \frac{9}{16}, 0.525, \frac{9}{20}$$

25 Answer

$$\frac{9}{16}, 55\%, 0.525, \frac{9}{20}$$

---

26 Comparing & Ordering Fractions, Decimals & Percents

Order the following from largest to smallest:

$$0.1492, \frac{1}{10}, 18\%, \frac{1}{8}$$

26 Answer

$$18\%, 0.1492, \frac{1}{8}, \frac{1}{10}$$

Comparing & Ordering Fractions, Decimals & Percents

Directions: Solve the problem using your knowledge of fractions, decimals, and percents.

---

27 Comparing & Ordering Fractions, Decimals & Percents

Order the following from largest to smallest:

$$38\%, \ \frac{7}{16}, \ 0.375, \ \frac{5}{8}$$

---

27 Answer

$$\frac{5}{8}, \ \frac{7}{16}, \ 38\%, \ 0.375$$

---

28 Comparing & Ordering Fractions, Decimals & Percents

Order the following from largest to smallest:

$$\frac{1}{5}, \ 54\%, \ \frac{1}{4}, \ 0.497$$

---

28 Answer

$$54\%, \ 0.497, \ \frac{1}{4}, \ \frac{1}{5}$$

---

29 Comparing & Ordering Fractions, Decimals & Percents

If 19 × 14 = 266, what is 1.9 × 0.14?

---

29 Answer

three decimal places to the left

0.266

Comparing & Ordering Fractions, Decimals & Percents

Directions: Solve the problem using your knowledge of fractions, decimals, and percents.

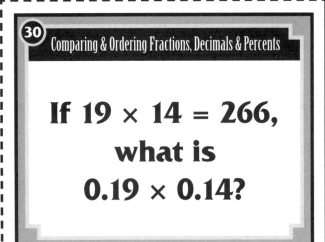

30
Comparing & Ordering Fractions, Decimals & Percents

If 19 × 14 = 266, what is 0.19 × 0.14?

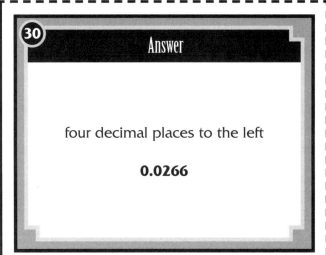

30
Answer

four decimal places to the left

0.0266

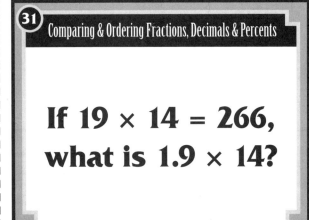

31
Comparing & Ordering Fractions, Decimals & Percents

If 19 × 14 = 266, what is 1.9 × 14?

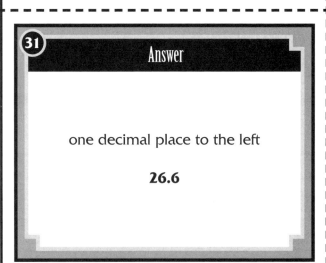

31
Answer

one decimal place to the left

26.6

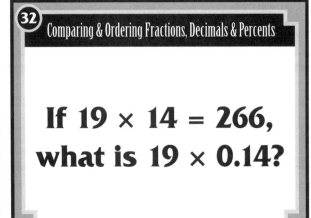

32
Comparing & Ordering Fractions, Decimals & Percents

If 19 × 14 = 266, what is 19 × 0.14?

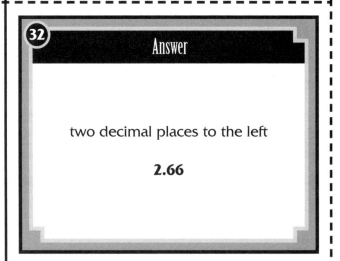

32
Answer

two decimal places to the left

2.66

Coordinate Pairs

Coordinate Pairs Quiz-Quiz-Trade cards reinforce students' conceptual understanding of all four quadrants of a coordinate grid, the *x* (horizontal) and *y* (vertical) axes, ordered pairs (including integers), the origin, and how to correctly identify and locate ordered pairs on a coordinate grid.

Sample Cards

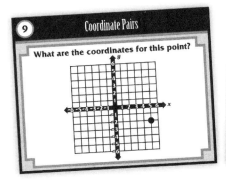

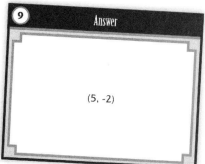

Coordinate Pairs

Directions: Use your knowledge of coordinate pairs to solve the problem.

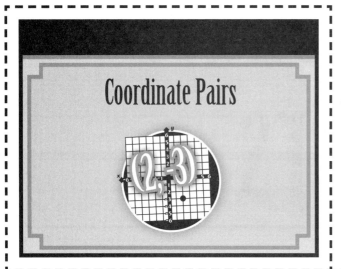

Coordinate Pairs

Card Set Label

When it's time to store this set, place this card label at the top of the set so that it's easy to identify for the next use.

1 Coordinate Pairs	1 Answer
(3, 4) is found in which quadrant?	Quadrant I

2 Coordinate Pairs	2 Answer
(-3, 4) is found in which quadrant?	Quadrant II

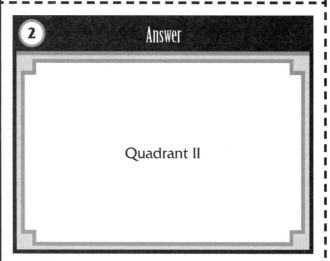

Coordinate Pairs

Directions: Use your knowledge of coordinate pairs to solve the problem.

3 Coordinate Pairs	**3** Answer
(-3, -4) is found in which quadrant?	Quadrant III
4 Coordinate Pairs	**4** Answer
(3, -4) is found in which quadrant?	Quadrant IV
5 Coordinate Pairs	**5** Answer
The coordinate pair (0, 0) is also known as the _____.	origin

Coordinate Pairs

Directions: Use your knowledge of coordinate pairs to solve the problem.

6 Coordinate Pairs	6 Answer
The vertical axis is also known as the ___ _____.	*y*-axis

7 Coordinate Pairs

What are the coordinates for this point?

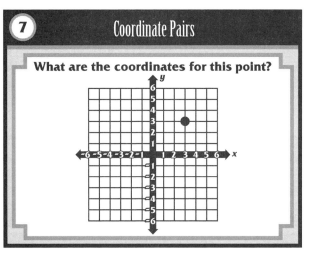

7 Answer

(3, 3)

8 Coordinate Pairs

What are the coordinates for this point?

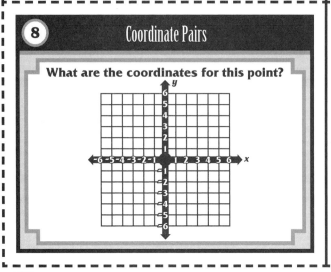

8 Answer

(0, 0)

Coordinate Pairs

Directions: Use your knowledge of coordinate pairs to solve the problem.

9 Coordinate Pairs	**9** Answer
What are the coordinates for this point? 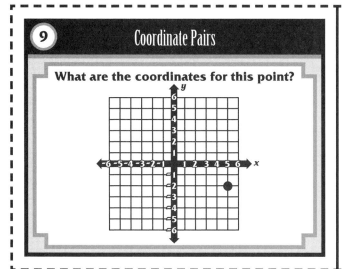	(5, -2)

10 Coordinate Pairs	**10** Answer
What are the coordinates for this point? 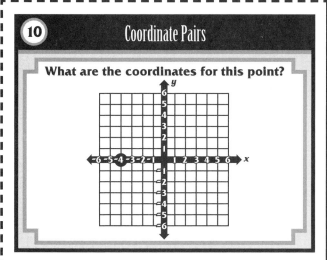	(-4, 0)

11 Coordinate Pairs	**11** Answer
What are the coordinates for this point? 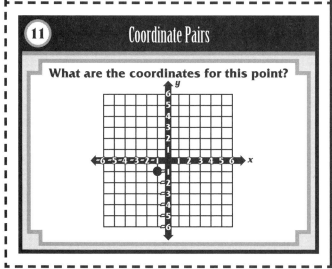	(-1, -1)

Coordinate Pairs

Directions: Use your knowledge of coordinate pairs to solve the problem.

12 Coordinate Pairs

What are the coordinates for this point?

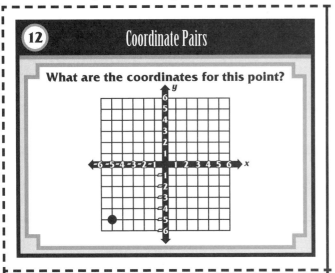

12 Answer

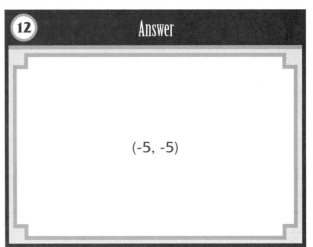

(-5, -5)

13 Coordinate Pairs

What are the coordinates for this point?

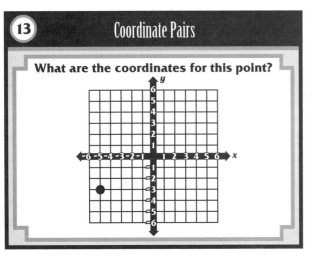

13 Answer

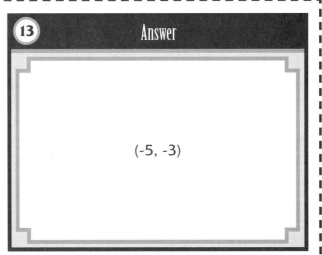

(-5, -3)

14 Coordinate Pairs

What are the coordinates for this point?

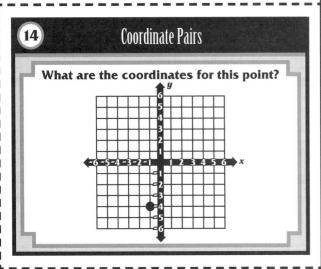

14 Answer

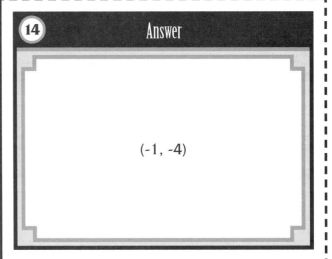

(-1, -4)

Quiz-Quiz-Trade: Middle School Math
Kagan Publishing · 800.933.2667 · www.KaganOnline.com

Coordinate Pairs

Directions: Use your knowledge of coordinate pairs to solve the problem.

15 Coordinate Pairs

What are the coordinates for this point?

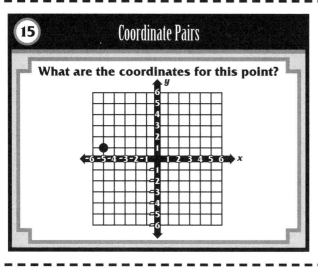

15 Answer

(-5, 1)

16 Coordinate Pairs

What are the coordinates for this point?

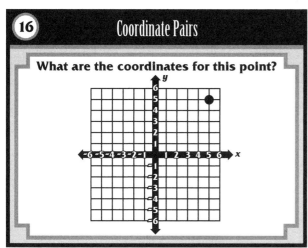

16 Answer

(5, 5)

17 Coordinate Pairs

What are the coordinates for this point?

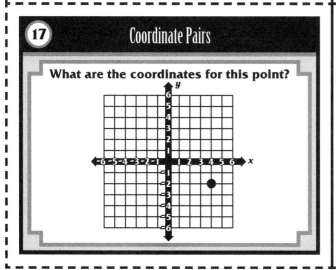

17 Answer

(4, -2)

Coordinate Pairs

Directions: Use your knowledge of coordinate pairs to solve the problem.

18 Coordinate Pairs	**18** Answer
What are the coordinates for this point? 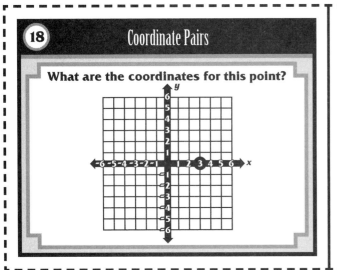	(3, 0)
19 Coordinate Pairs	**19** Answer
What are the coordinates for this point? 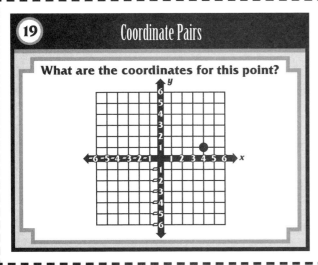	(4, 1)
20 Coordinate Pairs	**20** Answer
What are the coordinates for this point? 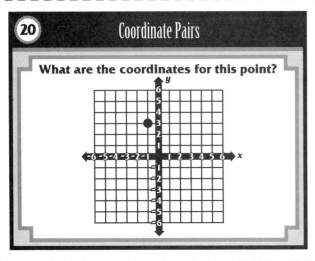	(-1, 3)

Coordinate Pairs

Directions: Use your knowledge of coordinate pairs to solve the problem.

21 Coordinate Pairs	**21** Answer
What are the coordinates for this point? 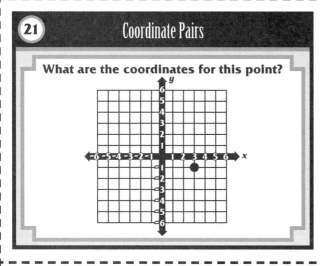	(3, -1)
22 Coordinate Pairs	**22** Answer
What are the coordinates for this point? 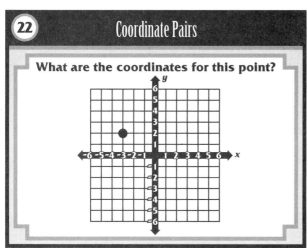	(-3, 2)
23 Coordinate Pairs	**23** Answer
What are the coordinates for this point? 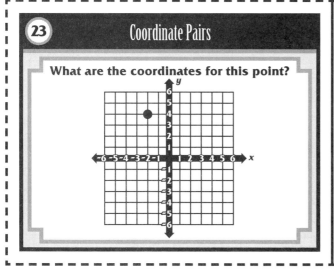	(-2, 4)

Coordinate Pairs

Directions: Use your knowledge of coordinate pairs to solve the problem.

24 Coordinate Pairs

What are the coordinates for this point?

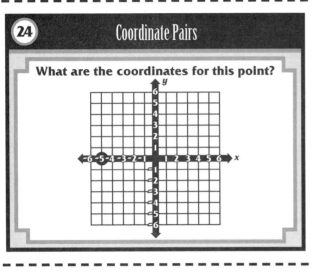

24 Answer

(-5, 0)

25 Coordinate Pairs

What are the coordinates for this point?

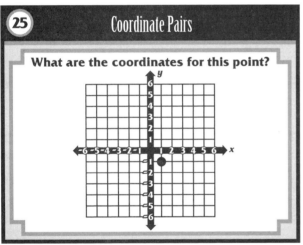

25 Answer

(1, -1)

26 Coordinate Pairs

What are the coordinates for this point?

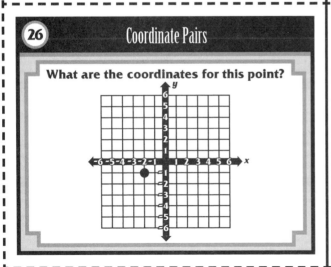

26 Answer

(-2, -1)

Coordinate Pairs

Directions: Use your knowledge of coordinate pairs to solve the problem.

27 | Coordinate Pairs

What are the coordinates for this point?

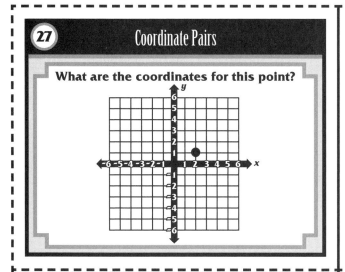

27 | Answer

(2, 1)

28 | Coordinate Pairs

What are the coordinates for this point?

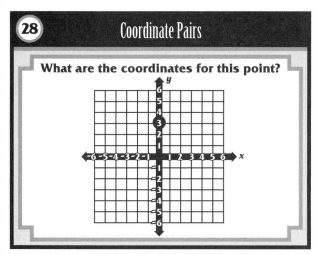

28 | Answer

(0, 3)

29 | Coordinate Pairs

What are the coordinates for this point?

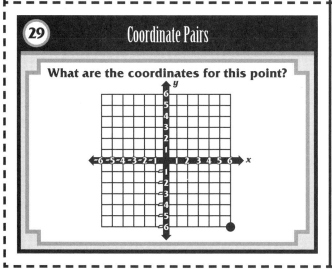

29 | Answer

(6, -6)

Coordinate Pairs

Directions: Use your knowledge of coordinate pairs to solve the problem.

30 Coordinate Pairs	**30** Answer
What are the coordinates for this point? 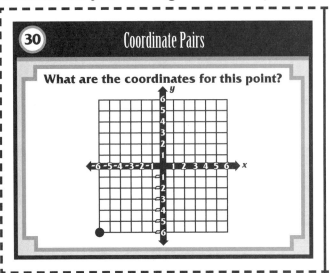	(-6, -6) 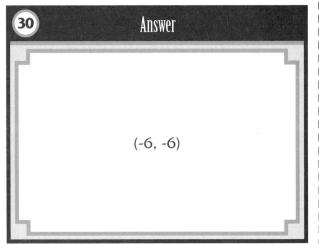
31 Coordinate Pairs	**31** Answer
What are the coordinates for this point? 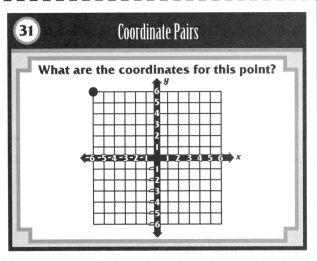	(-6, 6) 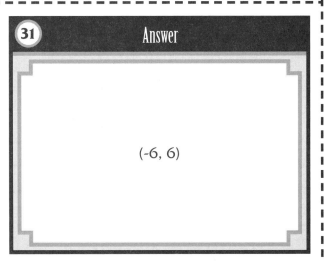
32 Coordinate Pairs	**32** Answer
What are the coordinates for this point? 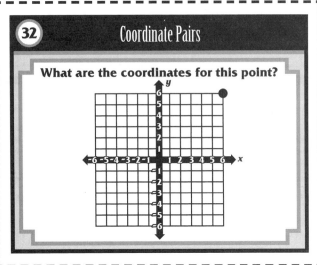	(6, 6) 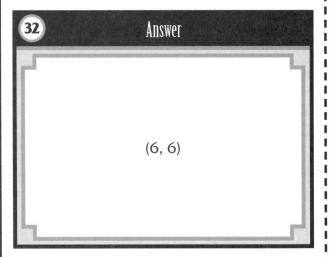

Data Analysis & Probability

What is the
95 92 87 85
81 77 75 57
Median?

Data Analysis & Probability Quiz-Quiz-Trade cards reinforce students' conceptual understanding of the different measures of central tendency; what is meant by continuous and discrete data, outliers, chance, and possible outcomes; and differentiating among impossible, independent, and certain events.

Sample Cards

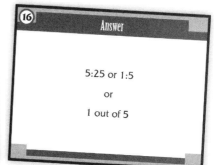

16	Data Analysis & Probability

A bag of marbles has 2 red, 4 green, 5 blue, 6 yellow, and 8 clear marbles. What is the probability of removing a blue marble?

16	Answer

5:25 or 1:5

or

1 out of 5

Data Analysis & Probability

Directions: Answer the question about data analysis and probability.

Data Analysis & Probability

Card Set Label

When it's time to store this set, place this card label at the top of the set so that it's easy to identify for the next use.

---

① Data Analysis & Probability

Define mean.

① Answer

The mean is the sum of a set of numbers divided by the number of numbers in the set.

---

② Data Analysis & Probability

Define median.

② Answer

The median is the middle number when numbers are arranged in numerical order. If there is an even number of data, determine the mean of the two middle numbers.

Data Analysis & Probability

What is the Median?

95 92 87 85 81 77 75 57

SET 5

Directions: Answer the question about data analysis and probability.

3 — Data Analysis & Probability

Define mode.

3 — Answer

The mode is the number (or numbers) that occurs most often in a set of data.

4 — Data Analysis & Probability

Define range.

4 — Answer

The range is the difference between the greatest and least numbers in a set of data.

5 — Data Analysis & Probability

What is a measure of central tendency?

5 — Answer

A measure of central tendency is a single value that attempts to describe a set of data by identifying the central position within that set of data.

Examples: mean, median, or mode

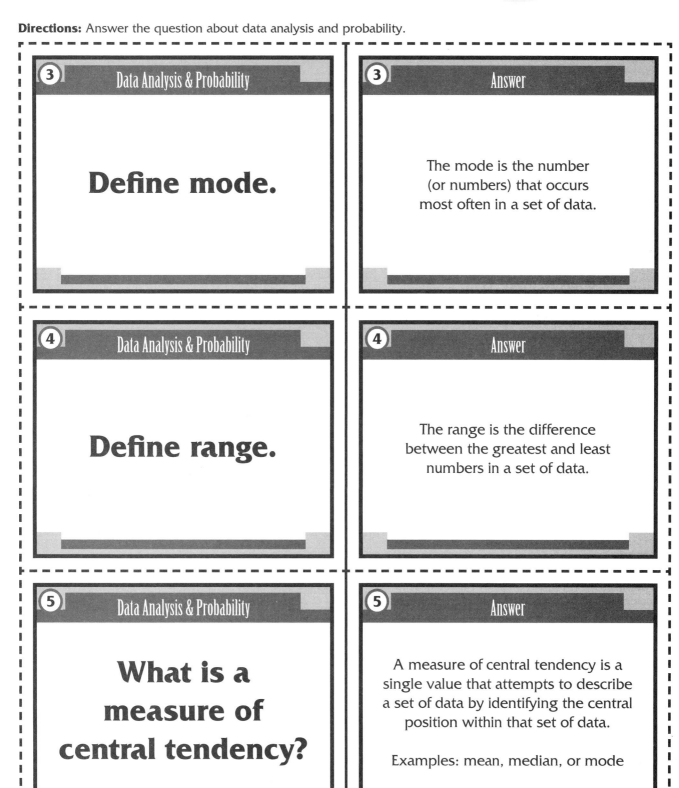

Data Analysis & Probability

Directions: Answer the question about data analysis and probability.

6 Data Analysis & Probability

Define average.

6 Answer

The average is a calculated "central" value of a set of numbers.

7 Data Analysis & Probability

Define outlier.

7 Answer

An outlier is a number in a set that is significantly different from the other numbers.

8 Data Analysis & Probability

Define chance.

8 Answer

Chance is a description of a probability expressed as a percent.

Example: 30% chance of precipitation

Data Analysis & Probability

What is the 95 92 87 85 81 77 75 57 Median?

Directions: Answer the question about data analysis and probability.

---

⑨ Data Analysis & Probability

What is an impossible event?

⑨ Answer

An impossible event is an event that will never occur; an event with probability = zero, or 0%.

---

⑩ Data Analysis & Probability

What are independent events?

⑩ Answer

Independent events are two events in which the result of one event does not depend on the result of the other event.

Example: flipping a coin and getting heads versus rolling a 5 on a 6-sided die

---

⑪ Data Analysis & Probability

What is a certain event?

⑪ Answer

A certain event is an event with probability = 1, or 100%.

Data Analysis & Probability

Directions: Answer the question about data analysis and probability.

---

12 Data Analysis & Probability

What are the mean, mode, and range for the following data?

2, 9, 5, 7, 5, 8, 5, 1, 3

(Use compatible sums to add these up.)

---

12 Answer

mean: $\frac{45}{9} = $ **5**

mode: **5**

range: $9 - 1 = $ **8**

---

13 Data Analysis & Probability

Ten students take a quiz. The mean score is 7. Using the following data, what could the missing scores be?

8, 10, 6, 9, 10, 5, 7, 5, □, □

(Use compatible sums to add these up.)

---

13 Answer

$10 \times 7 = 70$

sum of numbers = 60

$70 - 60 = 10$

any combination of two numbers that adds up to 10

---

14 Data Analysis & Probability

Using the following data, what is the median?

95, 92, 87, 85, 81, 77, 75, 74, 71, 65, 57

---

14 Answer

77

Quiz-Quiz-Trade: Middle School Math
Kagan Publishing • 800.933.2667 • www.KaganOnline.com

Data Analysis & Probability

Directions: Answer the question about data analysis and probability.

---

15 Data Analysis & Probability

Using the following data, what is the median?

95, 92, 87, 85, 81, 76, 72, 71, 69, 68, 65, 57

---

15 Answer

$$\frac{76 + 72}{2} = \frac{148}{2} = 74$$

---

16 Data Analysis & Probability

A bag of marbles has 2 red, 4 green, 5 blue, 6 yellow, and 8 clear marbles. What is the probability of removing a blue marble?

---

16 Answer

5:25 or 1:5

or

1 out of 5

---

17 Data Analysis & Probability

A bag of marbles has 2 red, 4 green, 5 blue, 6 yellow, and 8 clear marbles. What is the probability of removing a black marble?

---

17 Answer

0:25

or

no chance

Data Analysis & Probability

Directions: Answer the question about data analysis and probability.

---

18 Data Analysis & Probability.

A bag of marbles has 2 red, 4 green, 5 blue, 6 yellow, and 8 clear marbles. What is the probability of removing a red marble?

18 Answer

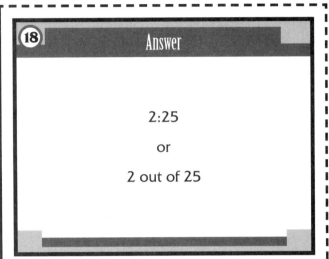

2:25

or

2 out of 25

---

19 Data Analysis & Probability

A 6-sided number cube is rolled. What is the probability of rolling an odd number?

19 Answer

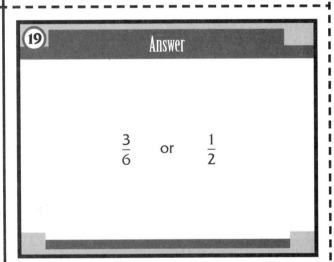

$\frac{3}{6}$ or $\frac{1}{2}$

---

20 Data Analysis & Probability

A 6-sided number cube is rolled. What is the probability of rolling a number greater than 4?

20 Answer

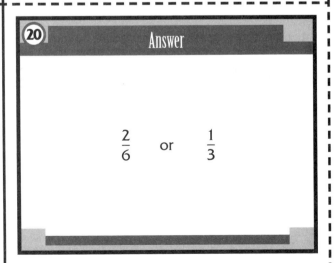

$\frac{2}{6}$ or $\frac{1}{3}$

Data Analysis & Probability

Directions: Answer the question about data analysis and probability.

---

21 Data Analysis & Probability

A deck of 52 cards is cut. What is the probability of cutting a jack? A red jack? The jack of hearts?

21 Answer

jack: $\frac{4}{52}$ or $\frac{1}{13}$

red jack: $\frac{2}{52}$ or $\frac{1}{26}$

jack of hearts: $\frac{1}{52}$

---

22 Data Analysis & Probability

This measure of central tendency is best used if data is skewed; it is less affected by outliers. It is used for data that involves ranking or rating.

22 Answer

median

---

23 Data Analysis & Probability

This measure of central tendency is best used if data is not skewed; it is most affected by outliers. It is often used for data such as test scores.

23 Answer

mean

Data Analysis & Probability

Directions: Answer the question about data analysis and probability.

(24) Data Analysis & Probability

This measure of central tendency is best used if data is discrete, such as gender or hair color; its downfall occurs when groups of scores are not near the center. The answer can have more than one value.

(24) Answer

mode

(25) Data Analysis & Probability

_____ _____ is data that can be counted; for example, the number of students in a class.

(25) Answer

discrete data

(26) Data Analysis & Probability

_____ _____ is data that can include any value between data points; for example, time and temperature.

(26) Answer

continuous data

 Quiz-Quiz-Trade: Middle School Math
Kagan Publishing • 800.933.2667 • www.KaganOnline.com

Data Analysis & Probability

Directions: Answer the question about data analysis and probability.

27 Data Analysis & Probability

Someone is guessing your birth month. What is the theoretical probability they will choose the correct month? Express your answer as a ratio.

27 Answer

1:12

28 Data Analysis & Probability

You roll a decahedron labeled 1 to 10. What is the theoretical probability of rolling a number greater than 3 and less than 8?

28 Answer

$\frac{4}{10}$ or $\frac{2}{5}$

29 Data Analysis & Probability

There are 52 cards in a deck. What is the theoretical probability of picking a 2 or 3 from the deck?

29 Answer

$\frac{8}{52}$ or $\frac{2}{13}$

Data Analysis & Probability

Directions: Answer the question about data analysis and probability.

30 Data Analysis & Probability

You roll a 6-sided die. What is the theoretical probability of rolling a number less than 4?

30 Answer

$\frac{3}{6}$ or $\frac{1}{2}$

31 Data Analysis & Probability

You have been asked to choose a letter at random from the word *Miramichi.* How many possible outcomes are there? What is the theoretical probability of choosing the letter *i*?

31 Answer

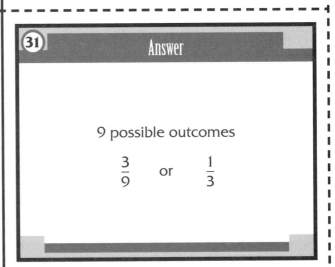

9 possible outcomes

$\frac{3}{9}$ or $\frac{1}{3}$

32 Data Analysis & Probability

You have been asked to choose a letter at random from the word *California.* How many possible outcomes are there? What is the theoretical probability of choosing a vowel?

32 Answer

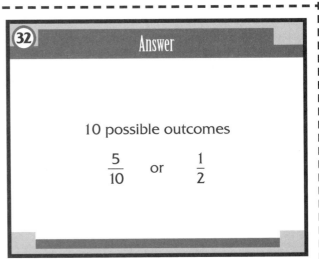

10 possible outcomes

$\frac{5}{10}$ or $\frac{1}{2}$

Quiz-Quiz-Trade: Middle School Math
Kagan Publishing · 800.933.2667 · www.KaganOnline.com

Divisibility Rules

Divisibility Rules Quiz-Quiz-Trade cards reinforce students' conceptual understanding of strategies used to determine whether or not certain numbers are divisible by others. These strategies help build upon student development of number sense.

Sample Cards

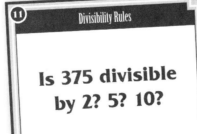

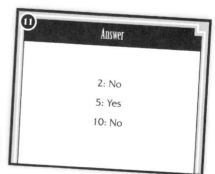

Divisibility Rules

Directions: Answer the question using your knowledge of divisibility rules.

Divisibility Rules

Card Set Label

When it's time to store this set, place this card label at the top of the set so that it's easy to identify for the next use.

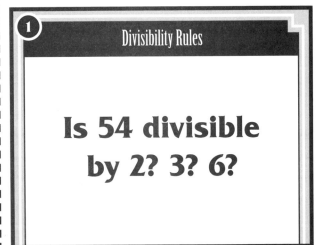

1 Divisibility Rules

Is 54 divisible by 2? 3? 6?

1 Answer

2: Yes

3: Yes

6: Yes

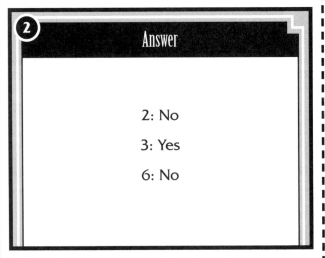

2 Divisibility Rules

Is 27 divisible by 2? 3? 6?

2 Answer

2: No

3: Yes

6: No

Divisibility Rules

Directions: Answer the question using your knowledge of divisibility rules.

3 | Divisibility Rules

Is 16 divisible by 2? 3? 6?

3 | Answer

2: Yes

3: No

6: No

4 | Divisibility Rules

Is 44 divisible by 2? 4? 8?

4 | Answer

2: Yes

4: Yes

8: No

5 | Divisibility Rules

Is 40 divisible by 2? 4? 8?

5 | Answer

2: Yes

4: Yes

8: Yes

Divisibility Rules

Directions: Answer the question using your knowledge of divisibility rules.

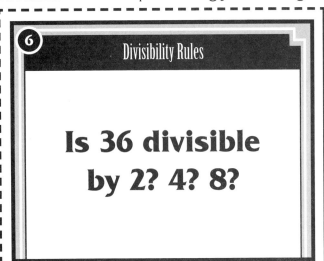

6 Divisibility Rules

Is 36 divisible by 2? 4? 8?

6 Answer

2: Yes

4: Yes

8: No

7 Divisibility Rules

Is 81 divisible by 3? 6? 9?

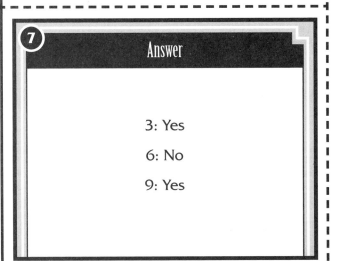

7 Answer

3: Yes

6: No

9: Yes

8 Divisibility Rules

Is 36 divisible by 3? 6? 9?

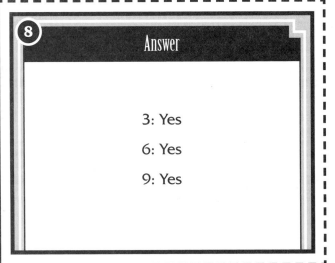

8 Answer

3: Yes

6: Yes

9: Yes

Quiz-Quiz-Trade: Middle School Math
Kagan Publishing • 800.933.2667 • www.KaganOnline.com

Divisibility Rules

Directions: Answer the question using your knowledge of divisibility rules.

---

⑨ Divisibility Rules

Is 24 divisible by 3? 6? 9?

⑨ Answer

3: Yes

6: Yes

9: No

---

⑩ Divisibility Rules

Is 840 divisible by 2? 5? 10?

⑩ Answer

2: Yes

5: Yes

10: Yes

---

⑪ Divisibility Rules

Is 375 divisible by 2? 5? 10?

⑪ Answer

2: No

5: Yes

10: No

Divisibility Rules

Directions: Answer the question using your knowledge of divisibility rules.

12 Divisibility Rules **Is 110 divisible by 2? 5? 10?**	**12** Answer 2: Yes 5: Yes 10: Yes
13 Divisibility Rules **Is 32 divisible by 2? 3? 4?**	**13** Answer 2: Yes 3: No 4: Yes
14 Divisibility Rules **Is 24 divisible by 2? 3? 4?**	**14** Answer 2: Yes 3: Yes 4: Yes

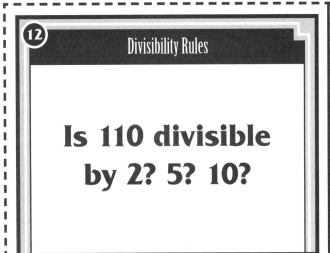
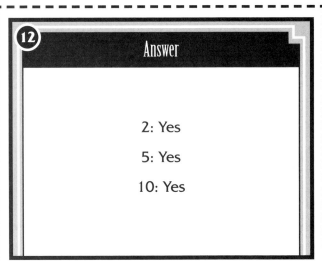
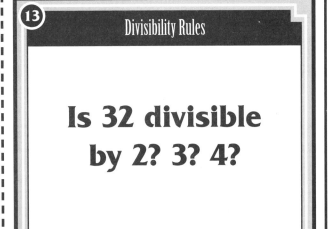
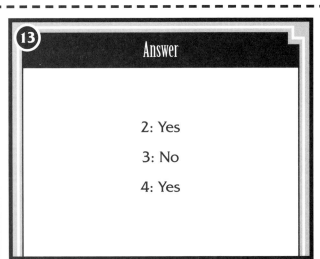
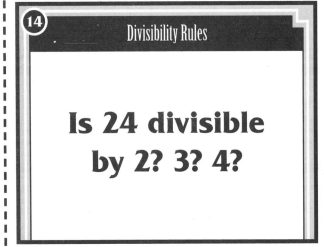
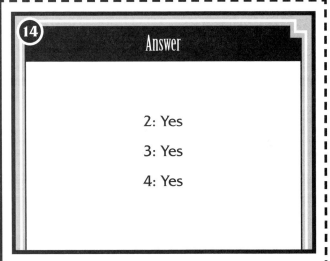

Quiz-Quiz-Trade: Middle School Math
Kagan Publishing · 800.933.2667 · www.KaganOnline.com

Divisibility Rules

Directions: Answer the question using your knowledge of divisibility rules.

15 Divisibility Rules	**15** Answer
Is 18 divisible by 2? 3? 4?	2: Yes 3: Yes 4: No
16 Divisibility Rules	**16** Answer
Is 105 divisible by 5? 6? 7?	5: Yes 6: No 7: Yes
17 Divisibility Rules	**17** Answer
Is 70 divisible by 5? 6? 7?	5: Yes 6: No 7: Yes

Divisibility Rules

Directions: Answer the question using your knowledge of divisibility rules.

18 Divisibility Rules	18 Answer
Is 42 divisible by 5? 6? 7?	5: No 6: Yes 7: Yes

19 Divisibility Rules	19 Answer
Is 180 divisible by 8? 9? 10?	8: No 9: Yes 10: Yes

20 Divisibility Rules	20 Answer
Is 120 divisible by 8? 9? 10?	8: Yes 9: No 10: Yes

Divisibility Rules

Directions: Answer the question using your knowledge of divisibility rules.

21 Divisibility Rules

Is 72 divisible by 8? 9? 10?

21 Answer

8: Yes

9: Yes

10: No

22 Divisibility Rules

Is 60 divisible by 3? 4? 5?

22 Answer

3: Yes

4: Yes

5: Yes

23 Divisibility Rules

Is 45 divisible by 3? 4? 5?

23 Answer

3: Yes

4: No

5: Yes

Divisibility
Rules

Directions: Answer the question using your knowledge of divisibility rules.

24   Divisibility Rules

Is 40 divisible by 3? 4? 5?

24   Answer

3: No

4: Yes

5: Yes

25   Divisibility Rules

Is 36 divisible by 4? 6? 8?

25   Answer

4: Yes

6: Yes

8: No

26   Divisibility Rules

Is 32 divisible by 4? 6? 8?

26   Answer

4: Yes

6: No

8: Yes

Divisibility Rules

Directions: Answer the question using your knowledge of divisibility rules.

27 — Divisibility Rules Is 18 divisible by 4? 6? 8?	**27 — Answer** 4: No 6: Yes 8: No
28 — Divisibility Rules Is 3 a factor of 152? 276?	**28 — Answer** 152: No 276: Yes
29 — Divisibility Rules Is 4 a factor of 56? 74?	**29 — Answer** 56: Yes 74: No

Divisibility Rules

Directions: Answer the question using your knowledge of divisibility rules.

30 Divisibility Rules

Is 6 a factor of 42? 76?

30 Answer

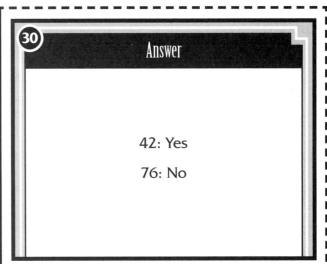

42: Yes

76: No

31 Divisibility Rules

Is 8 a factor of 128? 174?

31 Answer

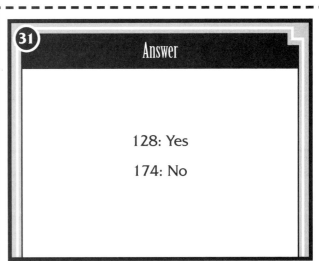

128: Yes

174: No

32 Divisibility Rules

Is 9 a factor of 683? 3,987?

32 Answer

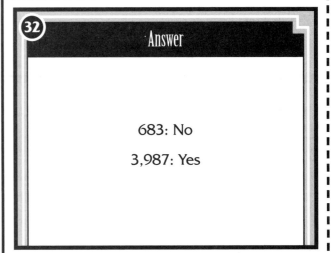

683: No

3,987: Yes

Exploring Circles & Area

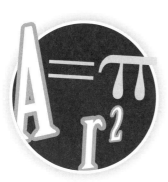

Exploring Circles & Area Quiz-Quiz-Trade cards reinforce students' conceptual understanding of the relationship among radius, diameter, and circumference; the relationship of circumference to pi; solving problems involving radius, diameter, and circumference; and developing and applying a formula for area of triangles, circles, and parallelograms.

Sample Cards

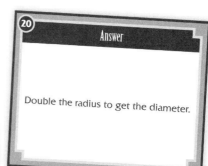

20 Exploring Circles & Area	20 Answer
If you know the radius of a circle, how would you find the diameter?	Double the radius to get the diameter.

Exploring Circles & Area

Directions: Answer the question using your circles and area knowledge.

Exploring Circles & Area

Card Set Label

When it's time to store this set, place this card label at the top of the set so that it's easy to identify for the next use.

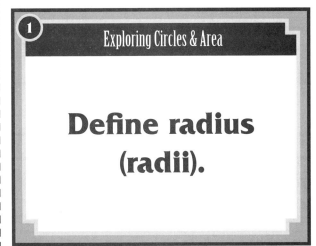

1 Exploring Circles & Area

Define radius (radii).

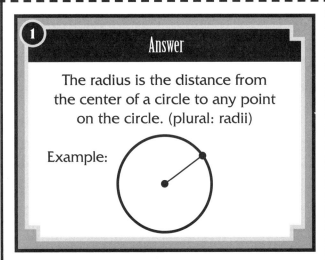

1 Answer

The radius is the distance from the center of a circle to any point on the circle. (plural: radii)

Example:

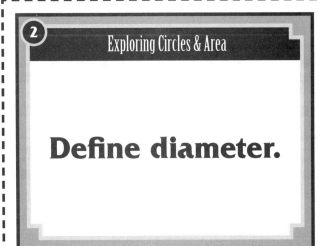

2 Exploring Circles & Area

Define diameter.

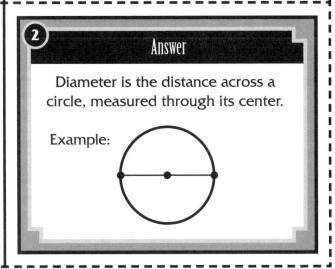

2 Answer

Diameter is the distance across a circle, measured through its center.

Example:

Quiz-Quiz-Trade: Middle School Math
Kagan Publishing · 800.933.2667 · www.KaganOnline.com

Exploring Circles & Area

Directions: Answer the question using your circles and area knowledge.

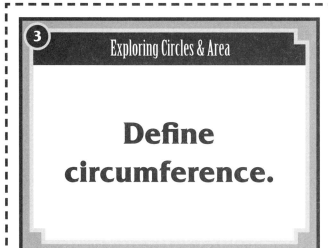

3 Exploring Circles & Area

Define circumference.

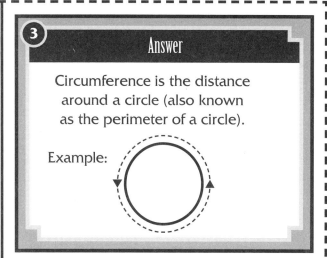

3 Answer

Circumference is the distance around a circle (also known as the perimeter of a circle).

Example:

4 Exploring Circles & Area

What is π?

4 Answer

π is the ratio of a circle's circumference to its diameter, equal to 3.14159265358979323846...

Example: an irrational number

5 Exploring Circles & Area

What is an irrational number?

5 Answer

An irrational number is a number that cannot be represented as a terminating or repeating decimal.

Example: π

Exploring Circles & Area

Directions: Answer the question using your circles and area knowledge.

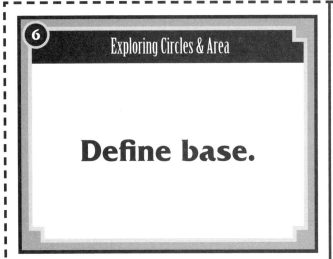

6 — Exploring Circles & Area

Define base.

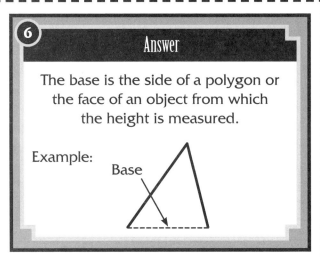

6 — Answer

The base is the side of a polygon or the face of an object from which the height is measured.

Example:

Base

7 — Exploring Circles & Area

Define height.

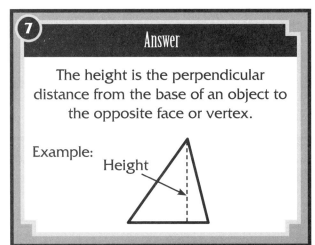

7 — Answer

The height is the perpendicular distance from the base of an object to the opposite face or vertex.

Example:

Height

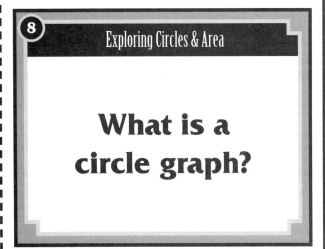

8 — Exploring Circles & Area

What is a circle graph?

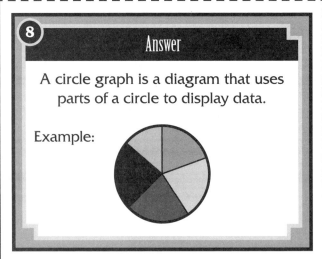

8 — Answer

A circle graph is a diagram that uses parts of a circle to display data.

Example:

Exploring Circles & Area

Directions: Answer the question using your circles and area knowledge.

---

9 — Exploring Circles & Area

What is a sector?

---

9 — Answer

A sector is a part of a circle between two radii and the included arc.

Example:

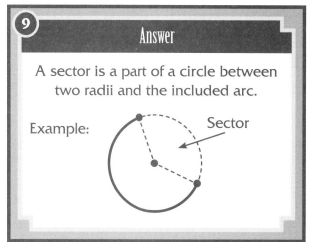

Sector

---

10 — Exploring Circles & Area

What is a legend?

---

10 — Answer

A legend is the part of a circle graph that shows what category each sector represents.

Example:

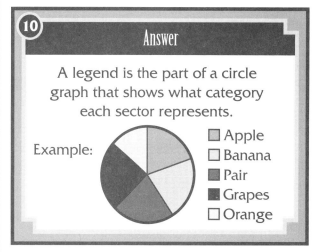

☐ Apple
☐ Banana
☐ Pair
☐ Grapes
☐ Orange

---

11 — Exploring Circles & Area

Define central angle.

---

11 — Answer

The central angle is the angle between the two radii that form a sector of a circle.

Example:

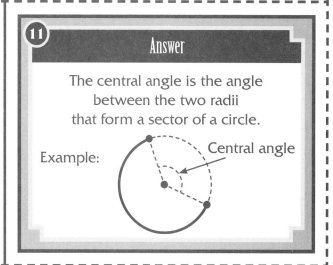

Central angle

Exploring Circles & Area

Directions: Answer the question using your circles and area knowledge.

12 Exploring Circles & Area

Why do we call π an irrational number?

12 Answer

π never repeats and never terminates.

13 Exploring Circles & Area

What is the formula for circumference?

13 Answer

$2\pi r$

or

πd

14 Exploring Circles & Area

A city park has a circular garden with a diameter of 20 meters. What is its area?

14 Answer

$A = \pi r^2$

$A = 3.14 \times 10^2$

$= 3.14 \times 100$

$= \textbf{314 m}^2$

Exploring Circles & Area

Directions: Answer the question using your circles and area knowledge.

---

15 | Exploring Circles & Area

A parallelogram has a base of 8.0 meters and a height of 3.5 meters. What is its area? What mental math strategy did you use?

---

15 | Answer

28 m²

Double Half

8 × 3.5

4 × 7

28

---

16 | Exploring Circles & Area

What is the formula for the area of a triangle?

---

16 | Answer

$$A = \frac{b \times h}{2}$$

---

17 | Exploring Circles & Area

How would you find the height of this triangle?

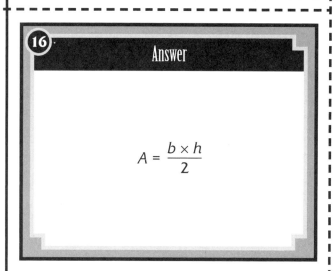

---

17 | Answer

Extend the base, so you can draw the perpendicular.

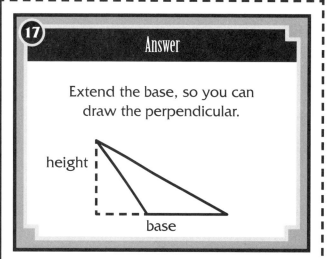

Exploring Circles & Area

Directions: Answer the question using your circles and area knowledge.

---

18 Exploring Circles & Area

The area of a triangle is 44 cm². If the base is 11 cm, what is the height?

18 Answer

$$Area = \frac{b \times h}{2}$$

$$44 = \frac{11 \times h}{2}$$

$$h = \textbf{8 cm}$$

---

19 Exploring Circles & Area

What is the formula for the area of a circle?

19 Answer

$$A = \pi r^2$$

---

20 Exploring Circles & Area

If you know the radius of a circle, how would you find the diameter?

20 Answer

Double the radius to get the diameter.

Exploring Circles & Area

Directions: Answer the question using your circles and area knowledge.

---

21 — Exploring Circles & Area

If you know the diameter of a circle, how would you find the radius?

21 — Answer

Halve the diameter to get the radius.

---

22 — Exploring Circles & Area

What are concentric circles?

22 — Answer

Concentric circles are circles that share the same center.

Example:

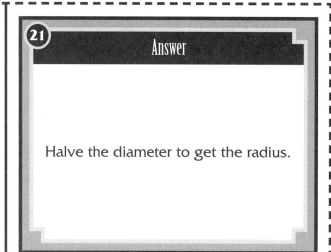

---

23 — Exploring Circles & Area

A circle graph shows the afterschool activities for students of a particular middle school. When we add up all the percents, what should they total?

23 — Answer

100%

Exploring Circles & Area

Directions: Answer the question using your circles and area knowledge.

---

24 Exploring Circles & Area

A circle graph shows the population of western states for a particular year. If CA is 44%, NV is 12%, and AZ is 34%, what percent is allotted to NM?

---

24 Answer

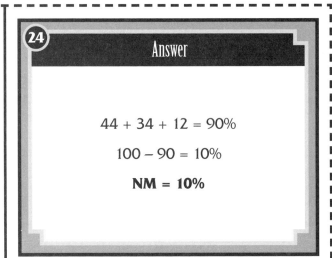

$44 + 34 + 12 = 90\%$

$100 - 90 = 10\%$

NM = 10%

---

25 Exploring Circles & Area

What is a line segment?

---

25 Answer

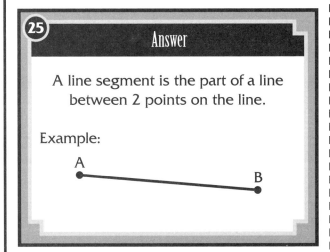

A line segment is the part of a line between 2 points on the line.

Example:

A ———————————— B

---

26 Exploring Circles & Area

If a sector angle of a circle graph represents 10% of something, how many degrees is this?

---

26 Answer

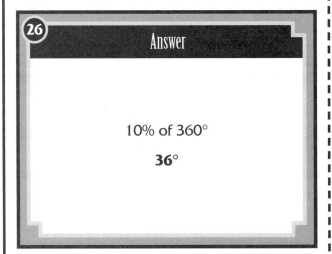

10% of 360°

36°

Exploring Circles & Area

Directions: Answer the question using your circles and area knowledge.

---

27 Exploring Circles & Area

The sum of the central angles of a circle is _____ % or _____ °

27 Answer

100% or 360°

---

28 Exploring Circles & Area

What is a perpendicular bisector?

28 Answer

A perpendicular bisector is a line which cuts a line segment into two equal parts at 90°.

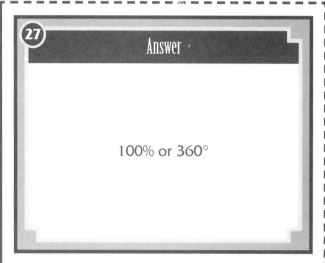

---

29 Exploring Circles & Area

What is a perpendicular line segment?

29 Answer

A line is perpendicular to another line if the two lines intersect at a right angle.

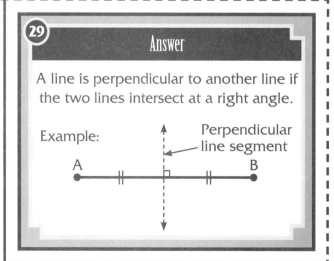

Quiz-Quiz-Trade: Middle School Math
Kagan Publishing • 800.933.2667 • www.KaganOnline.com

95

Exploring Circles & Area

Directions: Answer the question using your circles and area knowledge.

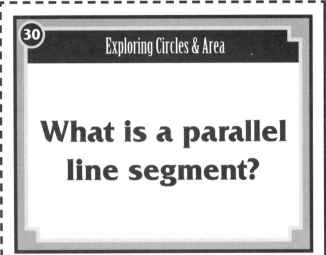

30 Exploring Circles & Area

What is a parallel line segment?

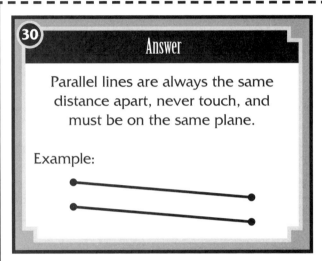

30 Answer

Parallel lines are always the same distance apart, never touch, and must be on the same plane.

Example:

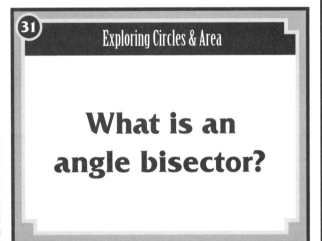

31 Exploring Circles & Area

What is an angle bisector?

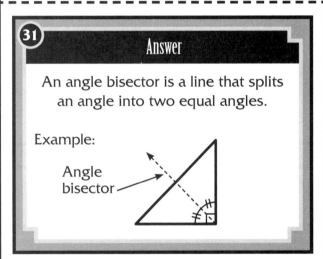

31 Answer

An angle bisector is a line that splits an angle into two equal angles.

Example:

Angle bisector

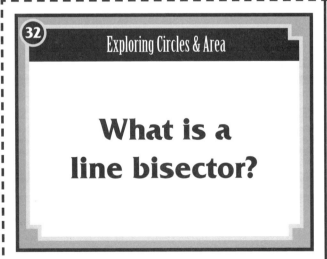

32 Exploring Circles & Area

What is a line bisector?

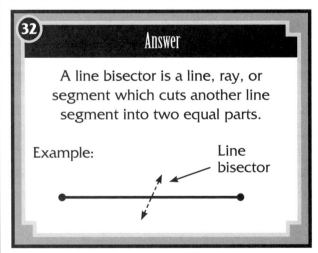

32 Answer

A line bisector is a line, ray, or segment which cuts another line segment into two equal parts.

Example:

Line bisector

Expressions & Equations

Expressions & Equations Quiz-Quiz-Trade cards reinforce students' conceptual understanding of the difference between expressions and equations, determining expressions to match word problems, modeling and solving one-step linear equations (including integers), evaluating expressions given the value of the variable(s), and the preservation of equality.

Sample Cards

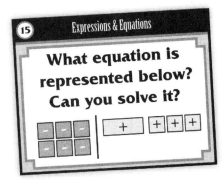

15 Expressions & Equations

What equation is represented below? Can you solve it?

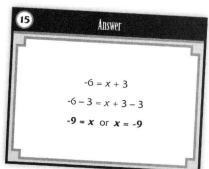

15 Answer

$-6 = x + 3$

$-6 - 3 = x + 3 - 3$

$-9 = x$ or $x = -9$

Expressions & Equations

Directions: Using your knowledge of expressions and equations, answer the question.

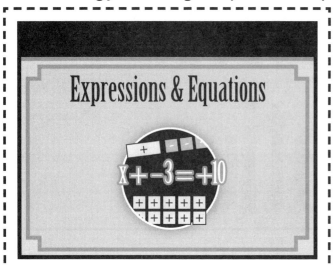

Expressions & Equations

Card Set Label

When it's time to store this set, place this card label at the top of the set so that it's easy to identify for the next use.

---

1 Expressions & Equations

What is a systematic trial?

1 Answer

A systematic trial is a way of solving an equation by choosing a value for the variable, then checking by substituting.

---

2 Expressions & Equations

What is the inspection method of solving an equation?

2 Answer

The inspection method is solving an equation by finding the value of the variable by using addition, subtraction, multiplication, and division facts.

Directions: Using your knowledge of expressions and equations, answer the question.

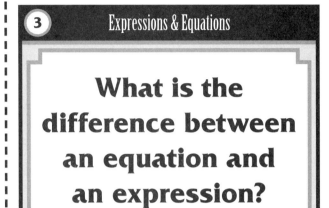

3 | Expressions & Equations

What is the difference between an equation and an expression?

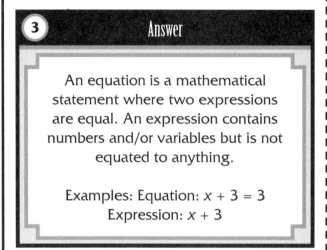

3 | Answer

An equation is a mathematical statement where two expressions are equal. An expression contains numbers and/or variables but is not equated to anything.

Examples: Equation: $x + 3 = 3$
Expression: $x + 3$

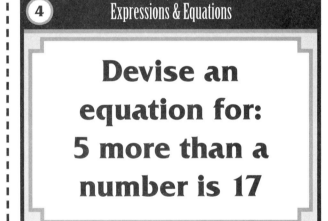

4 | Expressions & Equations

Devise an equation for: 5 more than a number is 17

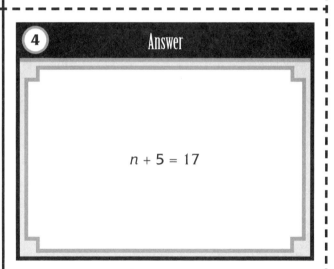

4 | Answer

$$n + 5 = 17$$

5 | Expressions & Equations

Devise an equation for: 4 less than a number is 15

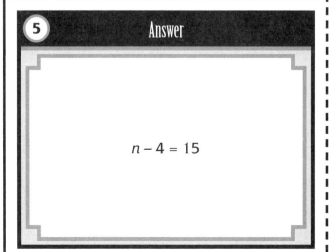

5 | Answer

$$n - 4 = 15$$

Expressions & Equations

Directions: Using your knowledge of expressions and equations, answer the question.

6 Expressions & Equations	6 Answer
Devise an equation for: 6 times a number is 42	$6n = 42$

7 Expressions & Equations	7 Answer
Devise an equation for: a number divided by 9 is 4	$\dfrac{n}{9} = 4$

8 Expressions & Equations	8 Answer
Devise an equation for: 2 more than 3 times a number is 23	$3n + 2 = 23$

Quiz-Quiz-Trade: Middle School Math
Kagan Publishing · 800.933.2667 · www.KaganOnline.com

Expressions & Equations

Directions: Using your knowledge of expressions and equations, answer the question.

---

9 Expressions & Equations

The side length of a regular octagon is 7 centimeters. Devise an equation to calculate the perimeter and solve.

9 Answer

$p = 8s$

$p = 8(7)$

$p = $ **56 cm**

---

10 Expressions & Equations

The perimeter of a square lawn is 36 meters. Devise an equation for perimeter and determine the length of the sides.

10 Answer

$p = 4s$

$36 = 4s$

$s = $ **9 cm**

---

11 Expressions & Equations

Create a word problem that matches:
$$\frac{n}{4} = 9$$

11 Answer

Answers will vary.

Sample answer: A bag of marbles is divided into 4 groups with 9 marbles in each group. How many marbles were in the bag?

x + −3 = +10

Expressions & Equations

Directions: Using your knowledge of expressions and equations, answer the question.

---

12 — Expressions & Equations

Create a word problem that matches: 7*n* = 28

12 — Answer

Answers will vary.

Sample answer: Twenty-eight cookies are divided among 7 children. How many cookies will each child get?

---

13 — Expressions & Equations

What is the inverse operation of division? Of multiplication?

13 — Answer

The inverse operation of division is multiplication; the inverse operation of multiplication is division.

---

14 — Expressions & Equations

What is the inverse operation of subtraction? Of addition?

14 — Answer

The inverse operation of subtraction is addition; the inverse operation of addition is subtraction.

Expressions & Equations

Directions: Using your knowledge of expressions and equations, answer the question.

15 Expressions & Equations	**15** Answer
What equation is represented below? Can you solve it? 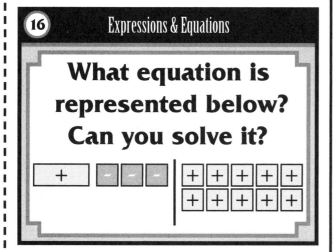	$-6 = x + 3$ $-6 - 3 = x + 3 - 3$ **$-9 = x$ or $x = -9$**
16 Expressions & Equations	**16** Answer
What equation is represented below? Can you solve it? 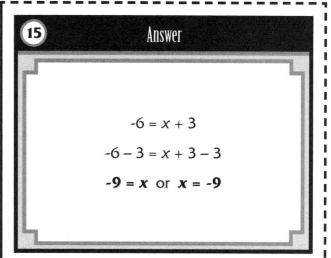	$x - 3 = +10$ $x - 3 + 3 = +10 + 3$ **$x = +13$**
17 Expressions & Equations	**17** Answer
What equation is represented below? Can you solve it? 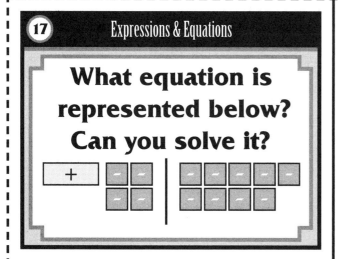	$x - 4 = -9$ $x - 4 + 4 = -9 + 4$ **$x = -5$**

Expressions & Equations

Directions: Using your knowledge of expressions and equations, answer the question.

---

18 — Expressions & Equations

What equation is represented below? Can you solve it?

$+$ $+$ $+$ $+$ | $+$ $+$ $+$
$+$ $+$ $+$

---

18 — Answer

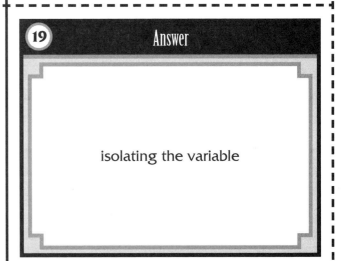

$$+7 = x + 2$$
$$+7 - 2 = x + 2 - 2$$
$$+5 = x \text{ or } x = +5$$

---

19 — Expressions & Equations

What is the key to solving any equation?

---

19 — Answer

isolating the variable

---

20 — Expressions & Equations

What is the first step to solve this equation algebraically?

$$n - 6 = 13$$

---

20 — Answer

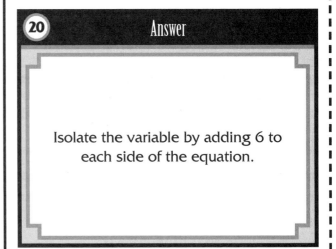

Isolate the variable by adding 6 to each side of the equation.

Expressions & Equations

Directions: Using your knowledge of expressions and equations, answer the question.

---

21 Expressions & Equations

What is the first step to solve this equation algebraically?

$$9 = 2n + 1$$

---

21 Answer

Isolate the variable by subtracting 1 from each side of the equation.

---

22 Expressions & Equations

The temperature dropped 7°F to -3°F. Devise an equation and determine the original temperature.

---

22 Answer

$$n - 7 = \text{-}3$$

$$n - 7 + 7 = \text{-}3 + 7$$

$$n = +4°F$$

---

23 Expressions & Equations

The temperature went from -9°F to +8°F. Devise an equation and determine the change in temperature.

---

23 Answer

$$\text{-}9 + n = +8$$

$$\text{-}9 + 9 + n = +8 + 9$$

$$n = +17°F$$

Expressions & Equations

Directions: Using your knowledge of expressions and equations, answer the question.

24 Expressions & Equations

Devise an equation for: 10 more than 3 times a number is 25

24 Answer

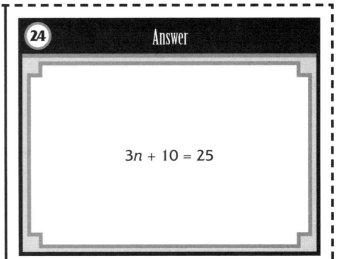

$3n + 10 = 25$

25 Expressions & Equations

Devise an equation for: 15 more than 6 times a number is 39

25 Answer

$6n + 15 = 39$

26 Expressions & Equations

What operation is necessary to solve for *n*?

$$\frac{n}{4} = 9$$

26 Answer

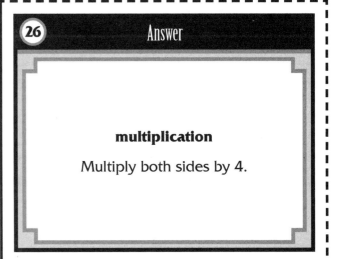

multiplication

Multiply both sides by 4.

Expressions & Equations

Directions: Using your knowledge of expressions and equations, answer the question.

---

27   Expressions & Equations

What operation is necessary to solve for *n*?

$$7n = 28$$

---

27   Answer

division

Divide both sides by 7.

---

28   Expressions & Equations

What is an expression?

---

28   Answer

An expression is a mathematical statement with numbers, operations $(+, -, \times, \div)$, and possibly variables that is not equated to something.

Example: $3 \times n - 2$

---

29   Expressions & Equations

What is an equation?

---

29   Answer

An equation is a mathematical statement with numbers, operations $(+, -, \times, \div)$, and possibly variables that is equated to something.

Example: $6 + 3 \times n = 15$

Expressions & Equations

Directions: Using your knowledge of expressions and equations, answer the question.

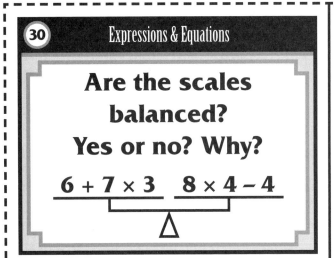

30 Expressions & Equations

Are the scales balanced?
Yes or no? Why?

$$6 + 7 \times 3 \qquad 8 \times 4 - 4$$

30 Answer

No

$6 + 7 \times 3 = 27$

$8 \times 4 - 4 = 28$

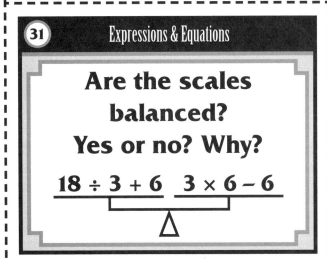

31 Expressions & Equations

Are the scales balanced?
Yes or no? Why?

$$18 \div 3 + 6 \qquad 3 \times 6 - 6$$

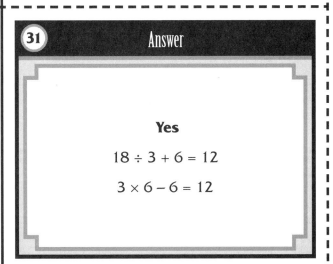

31 Answer

Yes

$18 \div 3 + 6 = 12$

$3 \times 6 - 6 = 12$

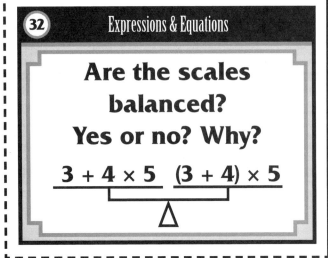

32 Expressions & Equations

Are the scales balanced?
Yes or no? Why?

$$3 + 4 \times 5 \qquad (3 + 4) \times 5$$

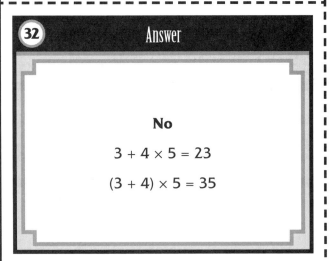

32 Answer

No

$3 + 4 \times 5 = 23$

$(3 + 4) \times 5 = 35$

Fractions—
Reinforcing
Addition

Fractions—Reinforcing Addition Quiz-Quiz-Trade cards reinforce students' conceptual understanding of determining the correct common denominator so that fractions with unlike denominators may be added.

Sample Cards

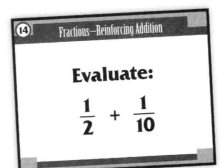

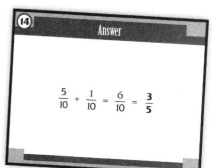

Fractions—Reinforcing Addition

Directions: Add the fractions, first finding the common denominator.

Fractions—Reinforcing Addition

When it's time to store this set, place this card label at the top of the set so that it's easy to identify for the next use.

---

1 Fractions—Reinforcing Addition

Evaluate:

$$\frac{1}{2} + \frac{1}{3}$$

1 Answer

$$\frac{3}{6} + \frac{2}{6} = \frac{5}{6}$$

---

2 Fractions—Reinforcing Addition

Evaluate:

$$\frac{1}{2} + \frac{2}{3}$$

2 Answer

$$\frac{3}{6} + \frac{4}{6} = \frac{7}{6} = 1\frac{1}{6}$$

Fractions—Reinforcing Addition

Directions: Add the fractions, first finding the common denominator.

3 Fractions—Reinforcing Addition

Evaluate:

$$\frac{1}{2} + \frac{1}{4}$$

3 Answer

$$\frac{2}{4} + \frac{1}{4} = \frac{3}{4}$$

4 Fractions—Reinforcing Addition

Evaluate:

$$\frac{1}{2} + \frac{3}{4}$$

4 Answer

$$\frac{2}{4} + \frac{3}{4} = \frac{5}{4} = 1\frac{1}{4}$$

5 Fractions—Reinforcing Addition

Evaluate:

$$\frac{1}{2} + \frac{1}{5}$$

5 Answer

$$\frac{5}{10} + \frac{2}{10} = \frac{7}{10}$$

Fractions—Reinforcing Addition

Directions: Add the fractions, first finding the common denominator.

6 Fractions—Reinforcing Addition

Evaluate:

$$\frac{1}{2} + \frac{3}{5}$$

6 Answer

$$\frac{5}{10} + \frac{6}{10} = \frac{11}{10} = 1\frac{1}{10}$$

7 Fractions—Reinforcing Addition

Evaluate:

$$\frac{1}{2} + \frac{1}{6}$$

7 Answer

$$\frac{3}{6} + \frac{1}{6} = \frac{4}{6} = \frac{2}{3}$$

8 Fractions—Reinforcing Addition

Evaluate:

$$\frac{1}{2} + \frac{5}{6}$$

8 Answer

$$\frac{3}{6} + \frac{5}{6} = \frac{8}{6} = 1\frac{2}{6} = 1\frac{1}{3}$$

Fractions—Reinforcing Addition

Directions: Add the fractions, first finding the common denominator.

---

9 Fractions—Reinforcing Addition

Evaluate:

$$\frac{1}{2} \ + \ \frac{2}{7}$$

---

9 Answer

$$\frac{7}{14} \ + \ \frac{4}{14} \ = \ \frac{11}{14}$$

---

10 Fractions—Reinforcing Addition

Evaluate:

$$\frac{1}{2} \ + \ \frac{1}{8}$$

---

10 Answer

$$\frac{4}{8} \ + \ \frac{1}{8} \ = \ \frac{5}{8}$$

---

11 Fractions—Reinforcing Addition

Evaluate:

$$\frac{1}{2} \ + \ \frac{3}{8}$$

---

11 Answer

$$\frac{4}{8} \ + \ \frac{3}{8} \ = \ \frac{7}{8}$$

Fractions—Reinforcing Addition

Directions: Add the fractions, first finding the common denominator.

Fractions—Reinforcing Addition

Evaluate:

$$\frac{1}{2} + \frac{5}{8}$$

Answer

$$\frac{4}{8} + \frac{5}{8} = \frac{9}{8} = 1\frac{1}{8}$$

Fractions—Reinforcing Addition

Evaluate:

$$\frac{1}{2} + \frac{2}{9}$$

Answer

$$\frac{9}{18} + \frac{4}{18} = \frac{13}{18}$$

Fractions—Reinforcing Addition

Evaluate:

$$\frac{1}{2} + \frac{1}{10}$$

Answer

$$\frac{5}{10} + \frac{1}{10} = \frac{6}{10} = \frac{3}{5}$$

Quiz-Quiz-Trade: Middle School Math
Kagan Publishing · 800.933.2667 · www.KaganOnline.com

Fractions—Reinforcing Addition

Directions: Add the fractions, first finding the common denominator.

---

15 Fractions—Reinforcing Addition

Evaluate:

$$\frac{1}{3} + \frac{1}{4}$$

15 Answer

$$\frac{4}{12} + \frac{3}{12} = \frac{7}{12}$$

---

16 Fractions—Reinforcing Addition

Evaluate:

$$\frac{1}{3} + \frac{3}{4}$$

16 Answer

$$\frac{4}{12} + \frac{9}{12} = \frac{13}{12} = 1\frac{1}{12}$$

---

17 Fractions—Reinforcing Addition

Evaluate:

$$\frac{1}{3} + \frac{3}{5}$$

17 Answer

$$\frac{5}{15} + \frac{9}{15} = \frac{14}{15}$$

Fractions—Reinforcing Addition

Directions: Add the fractions, first finding the common denominator.

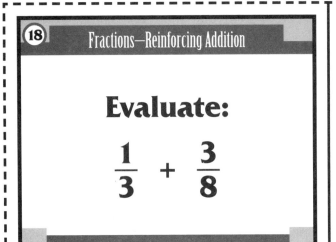

18 Fractions—Reinforcing Addition

Evaluate:

$$\frac{1}{3} + \frac{3}{8}$$

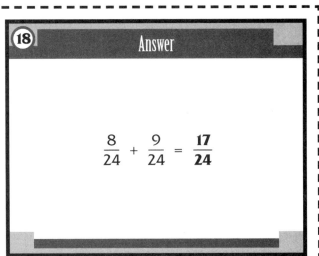

18 Answer

$$\frac{8}{24} + \frac{9}{24} = \frac{17}{24}$$

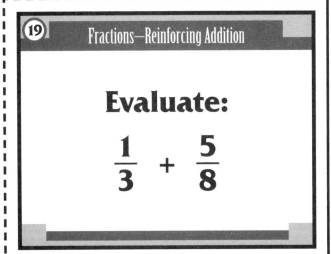

19 Fractions—Reinforcing Addition

Evaluate:

$$\frac{1}{3} + \frac{5}{8}$$

19 Answer

$$\frac{8}{24} + \frac{15}{24} = \frac{23}{24}$$

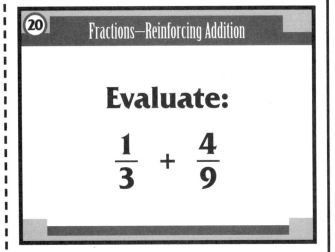

20 Fractions—Reinforcing Addition

Evaluate:

$$\frac{1}{3} + \frac{4}{9}$$

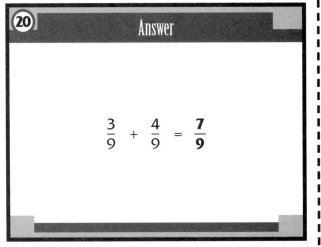

20 Answer

$$\frac{3}{9} + \frac{4}{9} = \frac{7}{9}$$

Fractions—Reinforcing Addition

Directions: Add the fractions, first finding the common denominator.

21 Fractions—Reinforcing Addition

Evaluate:
$$\frac{2}{3} + \frac{1}{6}$$

21 Answer

$$\frac{4}{6} + \frac{1}{6} = \frac{5}{6}$$

22 Fractions—Reinforcing Addition

Evaluate:
$$\frac{2}{9} + \frac{2}{3}$$

22 Answer

$$\frac{2}{9} + \frac{6}{9} = \frac{8}{9}$$

23 Fractions—Reinforcing Addition

Evaluate:
$$\frac{1}{4} + \frac{3}{5}$$

23 Answer

$$\frac{5}{20} + \frac{12}{20} = \frac{17}{20}$$

Fractions—Reinforcing Addition

Directions: Add the fractions, first finding the common denominator.

(24) Fractions—Reinforcing Addition

Evaluate:

$$\frac{1}{4} + \frac{1}{6}$$

(24) Answer

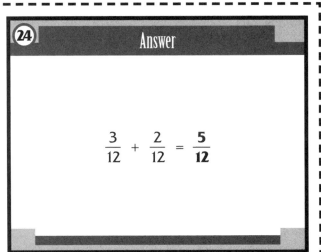

$$\frac{3}{12} + \frac{2}{12} = \frac{5}{12}$$

(25) Fractions—Reinforcing Addition

Evaluate:

$$\frac{1}{4} + \frac{3}{8}$$

(25) Answer

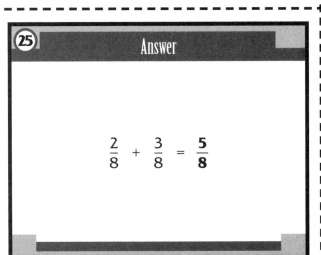

$$\frac{2}{8} + \frac{3}{8} = \frac{5}{8}$$

(26) Fractions—Reinforcing Addition

Evaluate:

$$\frac{1}{4} + \frac{7}{10}$$

(26) Answer

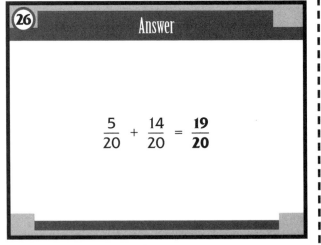

$$\frac{5}{20} + \frac{14}{20} = \frac{19}{20}$$

Fractions—Reinforcing Addition

Directions: Add the fractions, first finding the common denominator.

27 Fractions—Reinforcing Addition

Evaluate:

$$\frac{3}{4} + \frac{1}{5}$$

27 Answer

$$\frac{15}{20} + \frac{4}{20} = \frac{19}{20}$$

28 Fractions—Reinforcing Addition

Evaluate:

$$\frac{1}{5} + \frac{1}{6}$$

28 Answer

$$\frac{6}{30} + \frac{5}{30} = \frac{11}{30}$$

29 Fractions—Reinforcing Addition

Evaluate:

$$\frac{1}{5} + \frac{5}{8}$$

29 Answer

$$\frac{8}{40} + \frac{25}{40} = \frac{33}{40}$$

Fractions—Reinforcing Addition

Directions: Add the fractions, first finding the common denominator.

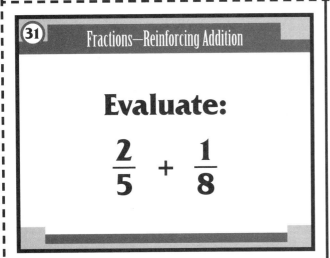

(30) Fractions—Reinforcing Addition

Evaluate:

$$\frac{1}{5} + \frac{3}{10}$$

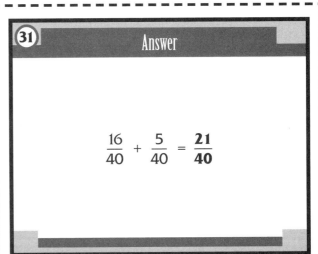

(30) Answer

$$\frac{2}{10} + \frac{3}{10} = \frac{5}{10} = \frac{1}{2}$$

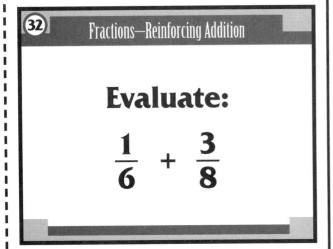

(31) Fractions—Reinforcing Addition

Evaluate:

$$\frac{2}{5} + \frac{1}{8}$$

(31) Answer

$$\frac{16}{40} + \frac{5}{40} = \frac{21}{40}$$

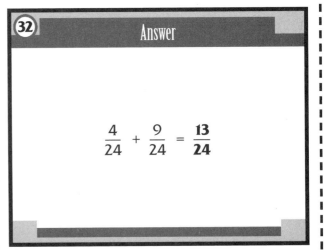

(32) Fractions—Reinforcing Addition

Evaluate:

$$\frac{1}{6} + \frac{3}{8}$$

(32) Answer

$$\frac{4}{24} + \frac{9}{24} = \frac{13}{24}$$

Fractions— Reinforcing Subtraction

Fractions—Reinforcing Subtraction Quiz-Quiz-Trade cards reinforce students' conceptual understanding of determining the correct common denominator so that fractions with unlike denominators may be subtracted.

Sample Cards

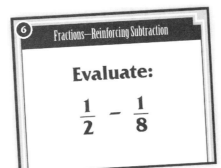

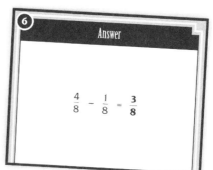

Fractions—Reinforcing Subtraction

Directions: Subtract the fractions, first finding the common denominator.

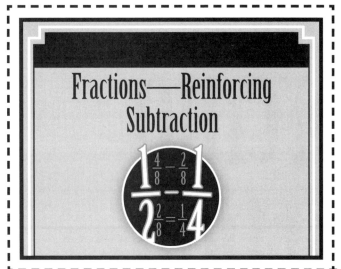

Card Set Label

When it's time to store this set, place this card label at the top of the set so that it's easy to identify for the next use.

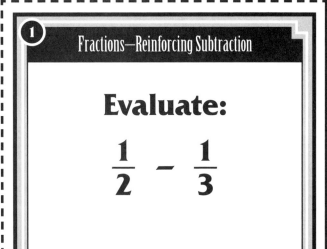

1 — Fractions—Reinforcing Subtraction

Evaluate:

$$\frac{1}{2} - \frac{1}{3}$$

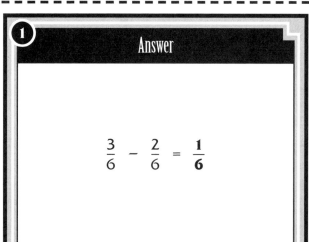

1 — Answer

$$\frac{3}{6} - \frac{2}{6} = \frac{1}{6}$$

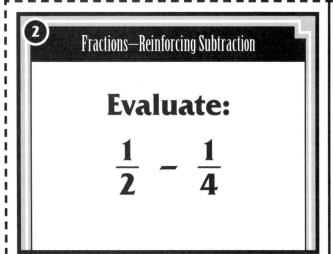

2 — Fractions—Reinforcing Subtraction

Evaluate:

$$\frac{1}{2} - \frac{1}{4}$$

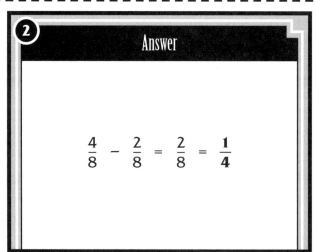

2 — Answer

$$\frac{4}{8} - \frac{2}{8} = \frac{2}{8} = \frac{1}{4}$$

Fractions—Reinforcing Subtraction

Directions: Subtract the fractions, first finding the common denominator.

---

3 Fractions—Reinforcing Subtraction

Evaluate:

$$\frac{1}{2} - \frac{2}{5}$$

---

3 Answer

$$\frac{5}{10} - \frac{4}{10} = \frac{1}{10}$$

---

4 Fractions—Reinforcing Subtraction

Evaluate:

$$\frac{1}{2} - \frac{1}{6}$$

---

4 Answer

$$\frac{3}{6} - \frac{1}{6} = \frac{2}{6} = \frac{1}{3}$$

---

5 Fractions—Reinforcing Subtraction

Evaluate:

$$\frac{1}{2} - \frac{2}{7}$$

---

5 Answer

$$\frac{7}{14} - \frac{4}{14} = \frac{3}{14}$$

Fractions—Reinforcing Subtraction

Directions: Subtract the fractions, first finding the common denominator.

---

6 Fractions—Reinforcing Subtraction

Evaluate:

$$\frac{1}{2} - \frac{1}{8}$$

6 Answer

$$\frac{4}{8} - \frac{1}{8} = \frac{3}{8}$$

---

7 Fractions—Reinforcing Subtraction

Evaluate:

$$\frac{1}{2} - \frac{3}{8}$$

7 Answer

$$\frac{4}{8} - \frac{3}{8} = \frac{1}{8}$$

---

8 Fractions—Reinforcing Subtraction

Evaluate:

$$\frac{1}{2} - \frac{2}{9}$$

8 Answer

$$\frac{9}{18} - \frac{4}{18} = \frac{5}{18}$$

Fractions—Reinforcing Subtraction

Directions: Subtract the fractions, first finding the common denominator.

---

9 Fractions—Reinforcing Subtraction

Evaluate:

$$\frac{1}{2} - \frac{3}{10}$$

---

9 Answer

$$\frac{5}{10} - \frac{3}{10} = \frac{2}{10} = \frac{1}{5}$$

---

10 Fractions—Reinforcing Subtraction

Evaluate:

$$\frac{1}{3} - \frac{1}{4}$$

---

10 Answer

$$\frac{4}{12} - \frac{3}{12} = \frac{1}{12}$$

---

11 Fractions—Reinforcing Subtraction

Evaluate:

$$\frac{2}{3} - \frac{1}{2}$$

---

11 Answer

$$\frac{4}{6} - \frac{3}{6} = \frac{1}{6}$$

Fractions—Reinforcing Subtraction

Directions: Subtract the fractions, first finding the common denominator.

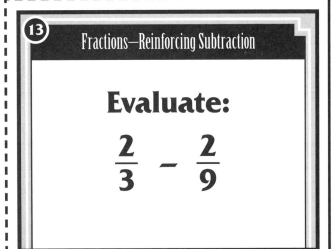

12 Fractions—Reinforcing Subtraction

Evaluate:

$$\frac{2}{3} - \frac{1}{6}$$

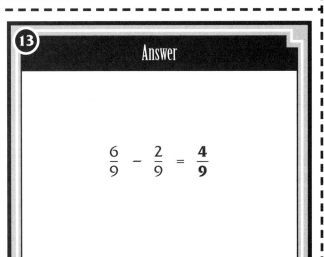

12 Answer

$$\frac{4}{6} - \frac{1}{6} = \frac{3}{6} = \frac{1}{2}$$

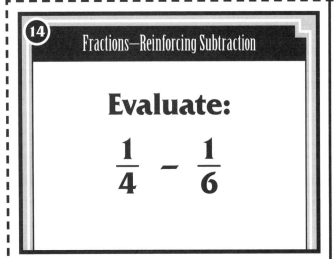

13 Fractions—Reinforcing Subtraction

Evaluate:

$$\frac{2}{3} - \frac{2}{9}$$

13 Answer

$$\frac{6}{9} - \frac{2}{9} = \frac{4}{9}$$

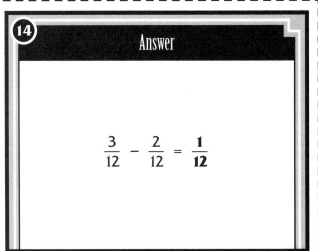

14 Fractions—Reinforcing Subtraction

Evaluate:

$$\frac{1}{4} - \frac{1}{6}$$

14 Answer

$$\frac{3}{12} - \frac{2}{12} = \frac{1}{12}$$

Quiz-Quiz-Trade: Middle School Math
Kagan Publishing · 800.933.2667 · www.KaganOnline.com

Fractions—Reinforcing Subtraction

Directions: Subtract the fractions, first finding the common denominator.

15 Fractions—Reinforcing Subtraction

Evaluate:

$$\frac{3}{4} - \frac{1}{2}$$

15 Answer

$$\frac{3}{4} - \frac{2}{4} = \frac{1}{4}$$

16 Fractions—Reinforcing Subtraction

Evaluate:

$$\frac{3}{4} - \frac{1}{3}$$

16 Answer

$$\frac{9}{12} - \frac{4}{12} = \frac{5}{12}$$

17 Fractions—Reinforcing Subtraction

Evaluate:

$$\frac{1}{5} - \frac{1}{6}$$

17 Answer

$$\frac{6}{30} - \frac{5}{30} = \frac{1}{30}$$

Fractions—Reinforcing Subtraction

Directions: Subtract the fractions, first finding the common denominator.

---

18 Fractions—Reinforcing Subtraction

Evaluate:

$$\frac{3}{5} - \frac{1}{2}$$

18 Answer

$$\frac{6}{10} - \frac{5}{10} = \frac{1}{10}$$

---

19 Fractions—Reinforcing Subtraction

Evaluate:

$$\frac{3}{5} - \frac{1}{3}$$

19 Answer

$$\frac{9}{15} - \frac{5}{15} = \frac{4}{15}$$

---

20 Fractions—Reinforcing Subtraction

Evaluate:

$$\frac{5}{6} - \frac{1}{2}$$

20 Answer

$$\frac{5}{6} - \frac{3}{6} = \frac{2}{6} = \frac{1}{3}$$

Fractions—Reinforcing Subtraction

Directions: Subtract the fractions, first finding the common denominator.

21 Fractions—Reinforcing Subtraction

Evaluate:

$$\frac{3}{8} - \frac{1}{3}$$

21 Answer

$$\frac{9}{24} - \frac{8}{24} = \frac{1}{24}$$

22 Fractions—Reinforcing Subtraction

Evaluate:

$$\frac{3}{8} - \frac{1}{4}$$

22 Answer

$$\frac{3}{8} - \frac{2}{8} = \frac{1}{8}$$

23 Fractions—Reinforcing Subtraction

Evaluate:

$$\frac{5}{6} - \frac{3}{8}$$

23 Answer

$$\frac{20}{24} - \frac{9}{24} = \frac{11}{24}$$

Fractions—Reinforcing Subtraction

Directions: Subtract the fractions, first finding the common denominator.

---

24 Fractions—Reinforcing Subtraction

Evaluate:

$$\frac{3}{8} - \frac{1}{6}$$

24 Answer

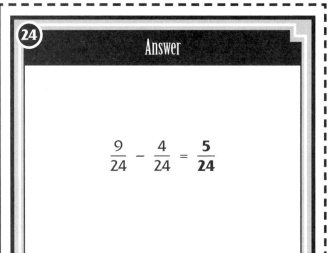

$$\frac{9}{24} - \frac{4}{24} = \frac{5}{24}$$

---

25 Fractions—Reinforcing Subtraction

Evaluate:

$$\frac{5}{8} - \frac{1}{2}$$

25 Answer

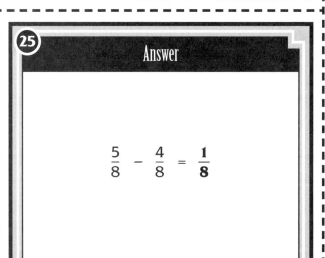

$$\frac{5}{8} - \frac{4}{8} = \frac{1}{8}$$

---

26 Fractions—Reinforcing Subtraction

Evaluate:

$$\frac{5}{8} - \frac{1}{3}$$

26 Answer

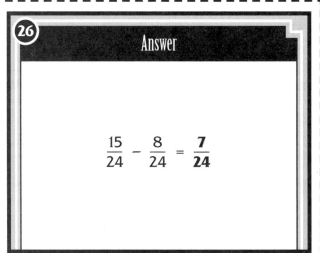

$$\frac{15}{24} - \frac{8}{24} = \frac{7}{24}$$

Fractions—Reinforcing Subtraction

Directions: Subtract the fractions, first finding the common denominator.

---

27 Fractions—Reinforcing Subtraction

Evaluate:

$$\frac{5}{8} - \frac{1}{4}$$

27 Answer

$$\frac{5}{8} - \frac{2}{8} = \frac{3}{8}$$

---

28 Fractions—Reinforcing Subtraction

Evaluate:

$$\frac{5}{7} - \frac{1}{3}$$

28 Answer

$$\frac{15}{21} - \frac{7}{21} = \frac{8}{21}$$

---

29 Fractions—Reinforcing Subtraction

Evaluate:

$$\frac{7}{8} - \frac{1}{4}$$

29 Answer

$$\frac{7}{8} - \frac{2}{8} = \frac{5}{8}$$

Fractions–Reinforcing Subtraction

Directions: Subtract the fractions, first finding the common denominator.

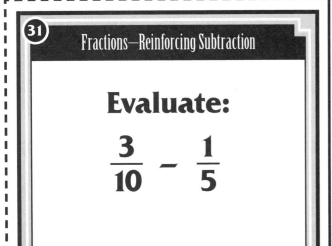

30 Fractions–Reinforcing Subtraction

Evaluate:

$$\frac{5}{9} - \frac{1}{3}$$

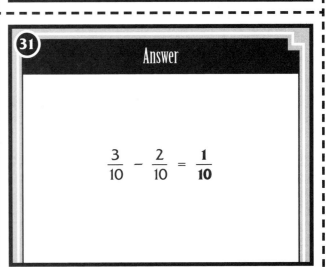

30 Answer

$$\frac{5}{9} - \frac{3}{9} = \frac{2}{9}$$

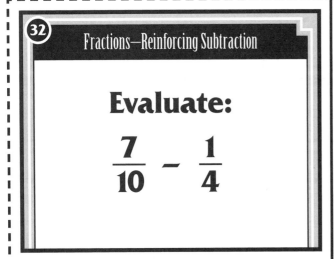

31 Fractions–Reinforcing Subtraction

Evaluate:

$$\frac{3}{10} - \frac{1}{5}$$

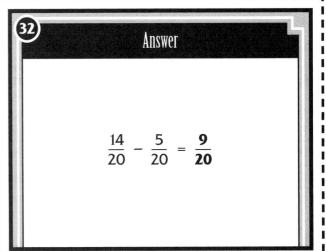

31 Answer

$$\frac{3}{10} - \frac{2}{10} = \frac{1}{10}$$

32 Fractions–Reinforcing Subtraction

Evaluate:

$$\frac{7}{10} - \frac{1}{4}$$

32 Answer

$$\frac{14}{20} - \frac{5}{20} = \frac{9}{20}$$

Integers— Modeling & Applying

Integers—Modeling & Applying Quiz-Quiz-Trade cards reinforce students' conceptual understanding of modeling positive and negative integers in real-life applications, opposite operations, and zero pairs.

Sample Cards

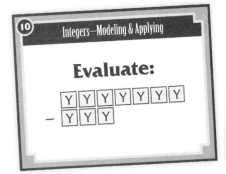

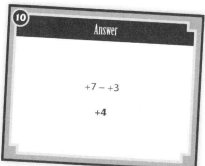

Integers—Modeling & Applying

Directions: Use your knowledge of integers to solve each problem.

Integers—Modeling & Applying

Evaluate

Card Set Label

When it's time to store this set, place this card label at the top of the set so that it's easy to identify for the next use.

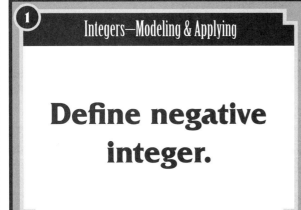

1 Integers—Modeling & Applying

Define negative integer.

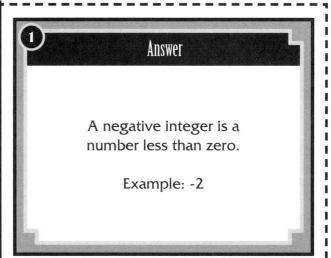

1 Answer

A negative integer is a number less than zero.

Example: -2

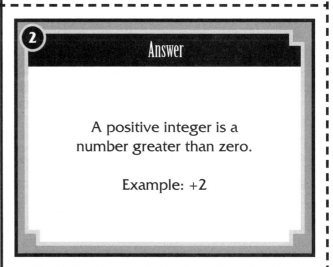

2 Integers—Modeling & Applying

Define positive integer.

2 Answer

A positive integer is a number greater than zero.

Example: +2

Integers—Modeling & Applying

Directions: Use your knowledge of integers to solve each problem.

3 Integers—Modeling & Applying

What is a zero pair?

3 Answer

A zero pair is two integers with a sum of zero.

Example: -2 and +2

4 Integers—Modeling & Applying

Define opposite integers.

4 Answer

Opposite integers are two opposite numbers whose sum is equal to zero.

Example: -3 and +3

5 Integers—Modeling & Applying

What is a yellow tile?

5 Answer

A yellow tile is used to model +1.

Example: | Y |

Integers—Modeling & Applying

Directions: Use your knowledge of integers to solve each problem.

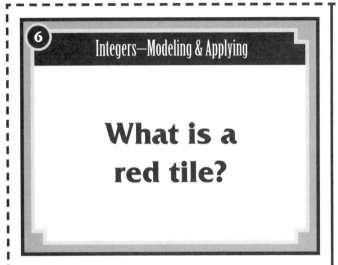

6 Integers—Modeling & Applying

What is a red tile?

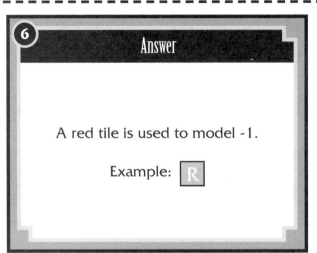

6 Answer

A red tile is used to model -1.

Example: R

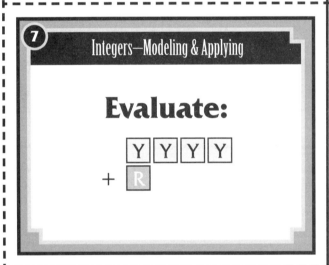

7 Integers—Modeling & Applying

Evaluate:

Y Y Y Y
+ R

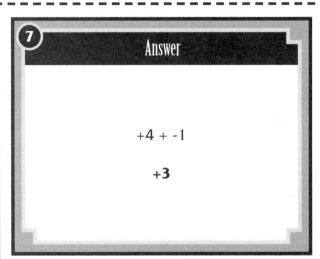

7 Answer

+4 + -1

+3

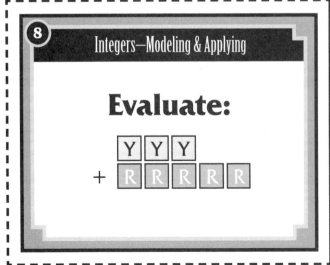

8 Integers—Modeling & Applying

Evaluate:

Y Y Y
+ R R R R R

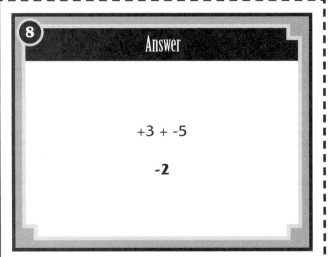

8 Answer

+3 + -5

-2

Integers—Modeling & Applying

Directions: Use your knowledge of integers to solve each problem.

9 Integers—Modeling & Applying

Evaluate:

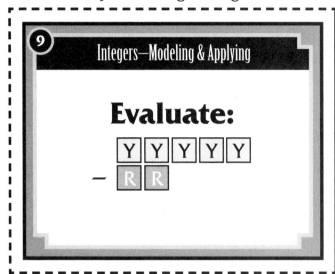

9 Answer

$+5 - -2$

+7

10 Integers—Modeling & Applying

Evaluate:

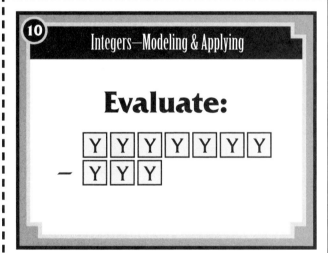

10 Answer

$+7 - +3$

+4

11 Integers—Modeling & Applying

Evaluate:

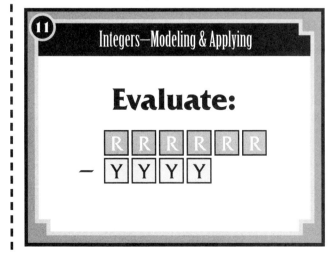

11 Answer

$-6 - +4$

-10

Integers—Modeling & Applying

Directions: Use your knowledge of integers to solve each problem.

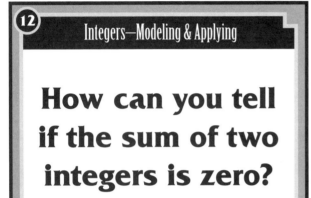

---

12 Integers—Modeling & Applying

How can you tell if the sum of two integers is zero?

12 Answer

same digit, different sign

13 Integers—Modeling & Applying

How can you tell if the sum of two integers is negative?

13 Answer

if both numbers are negative, or the negative number has the largest numerical value

---

14 Integers—Modeling & Applying

How can you tell if the sum of two integers is positive?

14 Answer

if both numbers are positive, or the positive number has the largest numerical value

---

Integers—Modeling & Applying

Directions: Use your knowledge of integers to solve each problem.

15 Integers—Modeling & Applying

How do you read -6 − +4 + -7?

15 Answer

"negative six minus positive four plus negative seven"

16 Integers—Modeling & Applying

The temperature is 5°F. Several hours later it drops to -3°F. How much did the temperature drop?

16 Answer

8°F

17 Integers—Modeling & Applying

The temperature is 8°F. Over a period of 12 hours, the temperature drops 14°F. What is the temperature now?

17 Answer

-6°F

Integers—Modeling & Applying

Directions: Use your knowledge of integers to solve each problem.

---

18 Integers—Modeling & Applying

The temperature in Minnesota is -12°F. The temperature in Michigan is 3°F. What is the difference in temperature?

18 Answer

15°F

---

19 Integers—Modeling & Applying

When you subtract two positive integers, is their difference always a positive integer?

19 Answer

No, not if the subtrahend (second number) has a larger numerical value their difference is not always a positive integer.

Example: +7 − +10 = -3

---

20 Integers—Modeling & Applying

Evaluate:

+1 + -5

20 Answer

-4

Integers—Modeling & Applying

Directions: Use your knowledge of integers to solve each problem.

21 Integers—Modeling & Applying

Evaluate:
+3 + -1

21 Answer

+2

22 Integers—Modeling & Applying

Evaluate:
-4 + +7

22 Answer

+3

23 Integers—Modeling & Applying

Evaluate:
-5 + +5

23 Answer

0

Integers—Modeling & Applying

Directions: Use your knowledge of integers to solve each problem.

24 Integers—Modeling & Applying

Evaluate:
-6 + +3

24 Answer

-3

25 Integers—Modeling & Applying

Evaluate:
-7 + -9

25 Answer

-16

26 Integers—Modeling & Applying

Evaluate:
-8 + -7

26 Answer

-15

Quiz-Quiz-Trade: Middle School Math
Kagan Publishing • 800.933.2667 • www.KaganOnline.com

Integers—Modeling & Applying

Directions: Use your knowledge of integers to solve each problem.

27 Integers—Modeling & Applying

Evaluate:
-9 + -5

27 Answer

-14

28 Integers—Modeling & Applying

Evaluate:
+1 – -5

28 Answer

+6

29 Integers—Modeling & Applying

Evaluate:
+2 – -3

29 Answer

+5

Integers—Modeling & Applying

Directions: Use your knowledge of integers to solve each problem.

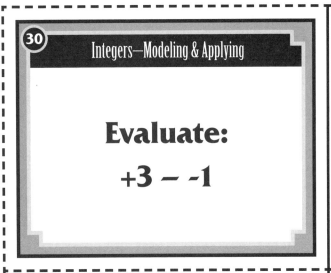

30 Integers—Modeling & Applying

Evaluate:

+3 – -1

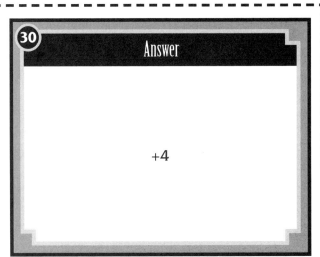

30 Answer

+4

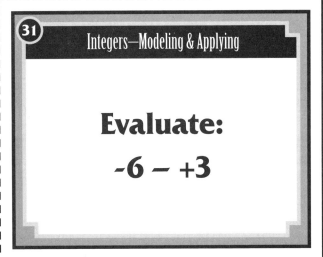

31 Integers—Modeling & Applying

Evaluate:

-6 – +3

31 Answer

-9

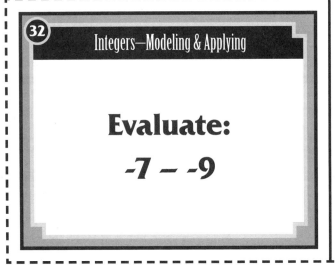

32 Integers—Modeling & Applying

Evaluate:

-7 – -9

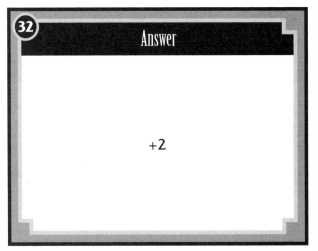

32 Answer

+2

Integers— Reinforcing Addition

Integers—Reinforcing Addition Quiz-Quiz-Trade cards reinforce students' conceptual understanding of adding positive and negative integers.

Sample Cards

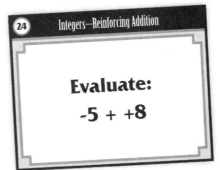

24 Integers—Reinforcing Addition

Evaluate:
-5 + +8

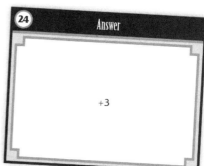

24 Answer

+3

Integers—Reinforcing Addition

Directions: Add the given integers.

Integers—Reinforcing Addition

Card Set Label

When it's time to store this set, place this card label at the top of the set so that it's easy to identify for the next use.

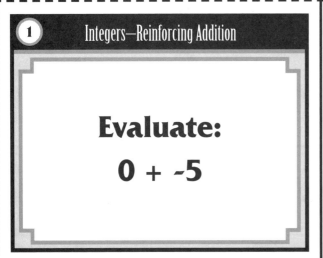

1 | Integers—Reinforcing Addition

Evaluate:

0 + -5

1 | Answer

-5

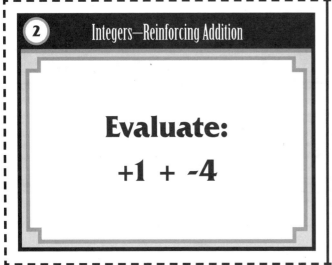

2 | Integers—Reinforcing Addition

Evaluate:

+1 + -4

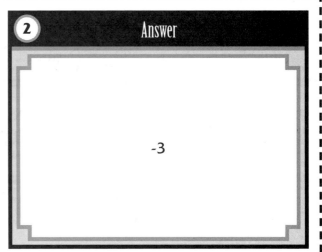

2 | Answer

-3

Integers—Reinforcing Addition

Directions: Add the given integers.

3 Integers—Reinforcing Addition

Evaluate:
+2 + -3

3 Answer

-1

4 Integers—Reinforcing Addition

Evaluate:
+3 + -2

4 Answer

+1

5 Integers—Reinforcing Addition

Evaluate:
+4 + -1

5 Answer

+3

Integers—Reinforcing Addition

Directions: Add the given integers.

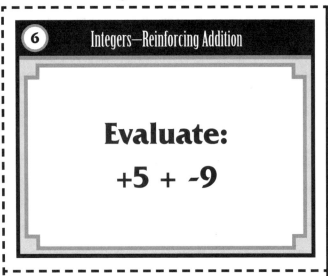

6 Integers—Reinforcing Addition

Evaluate:

+5 + -9

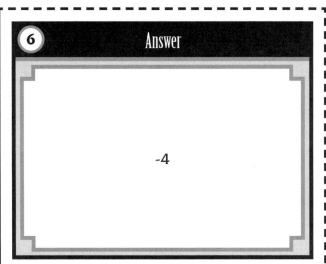

6 Answer

-4

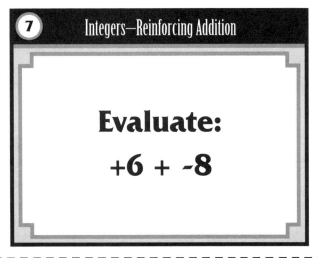

7 Integers—Reinforcing Addition

Evaluate:

+6 + -8

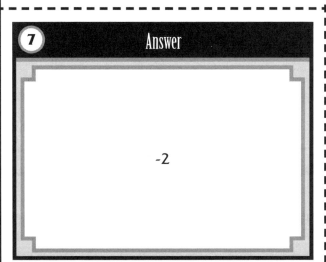

7 Answer

-2

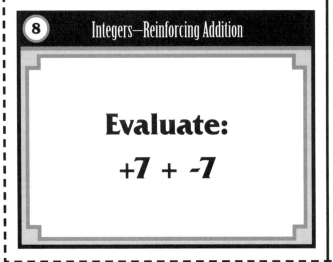

8 Integers—Reinforcing Addition

Evaluate:

+7 + -7

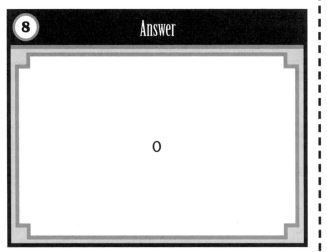

8 Answer

0

SET 12

Directions: Add the given integers.

9 Integers—Reinforcing Addition

Evaluate:

+8 + -6

9 Answer

+2

10 Integers—Reinforcing Addition

Evaluate:

+9 + -5

10 Answer

+4

11 Integers—Reinforcing Addition

Evaluate:

+1 + -2

11 Answer

-1

Integers—Reinforcing Addition

Directions: Add the given integers.

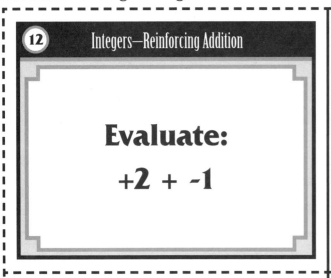

12 Integers—Reinforcing Addition

Evaluate:
+2 + -1

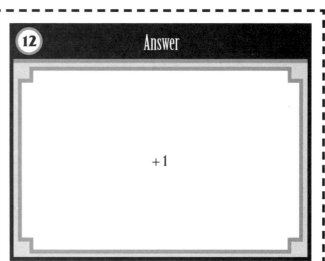

12 Answer

+1

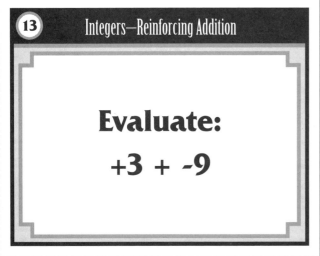

13 Integers—Reinforcing Addition

Evaluate:
+3 + -9

13 Answer

-6

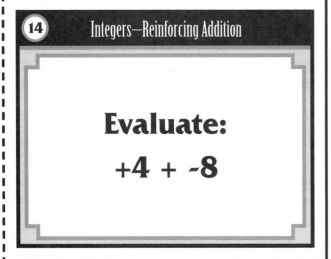

14 Integers—Reinforcing Addition

Evaluate:
+4 + -8

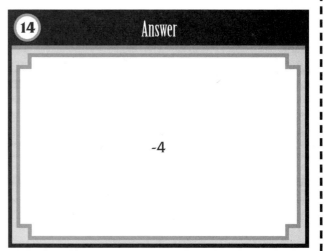

14 Answer

-4

Integers—Reinforcing Addition

Directions: Add the given integers.

15 Integers—Reinforcing Addition

Evaluate:
+5 + -7

15 Answer

-2

16 Integers—Reinforcing Addition

Evaluate:
+6 + -6

16 Answer

0

17 Integers—Reinforcing Addition

Evaluate:
+7 + -5

17 Answer

+2

Integers—Reinforcing Addition

Directions: Add the given integers.

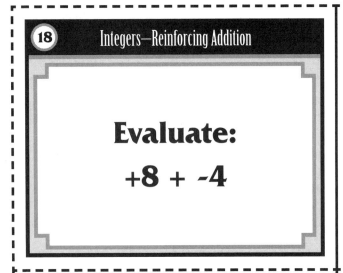

18 Integers—Reinforcing Addition

Evaluate:
+8 + -4

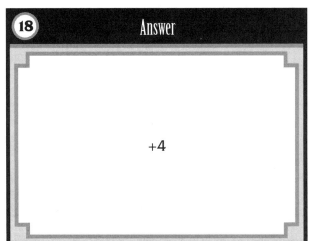

18 Answer

+4

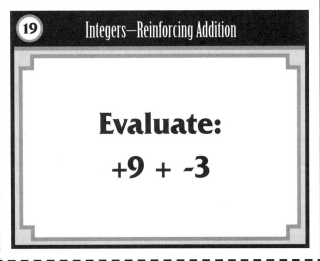

19 Integers—Reinforcing Addition

Evaluate:
+9 + -3

19 Answer

+6

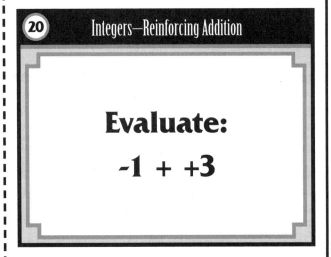

20 Integers—Reinforcing Addition

Evaluate:
-1 + +3

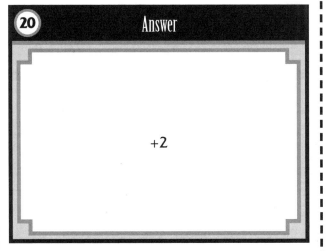

20 Answer

+2

Integers—Reinforcing Addition

Directions: Add the given integers.

21 Integers—Reinforcing Addition	**21** Answer
Evaluate: -2 + +2	0
22 Integers—Reinforcing Addition	**22** Answer
Evaluate: -3 + +1	-2
23 Integers—Reinforcing Addition	**23** Answer
Evaluate: -4 + +9	+5

Integers—Reinforcing Addition

Directions: Add the given integers.

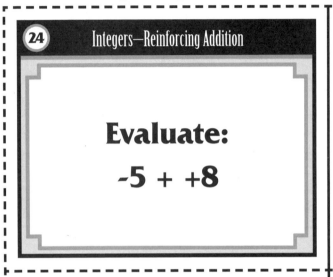

24   Integers—Reinforcing Addition

Evaluate:

-5 + +8

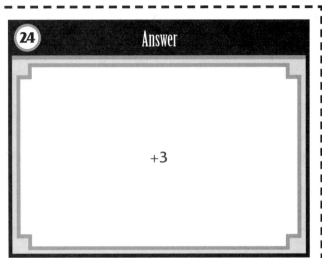

24   Answer

+3

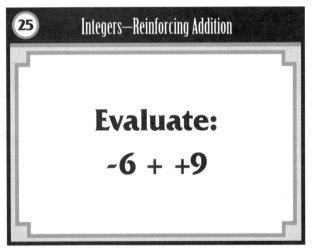

25   Integers—Reinforcing Addition

Evaluate:

-6 + +9

25   Answer

+3

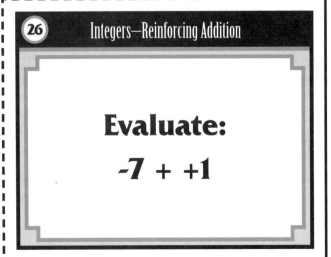

26   Integers—Reinforcing Addition

Evaluate:

-7 + +1

26   Answer

-6

Quiz-Quiz-Trade: Middle School Math
Kagan Publishing • 800.933.2667 • www.KaganOnline.com

Directions: Add the given integers.

27 Integers—Reinforcing Addition	**27** Answer
Evaluate: -8 + +5	-3
28 Integers—Reinforcing Addition	**28** Answer
Evaluate: -9 + +4	-5
29 Integers—Reinforcing Addition	**29** Answer
Evaluate: -2 + -8	-10

Integers—Reinforcing Addition

Directions: Add the given integers.

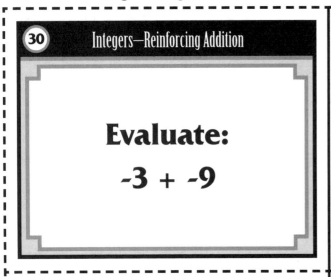

30 Integers—Reinforcing Addition

Evaluate:
-3 + -9

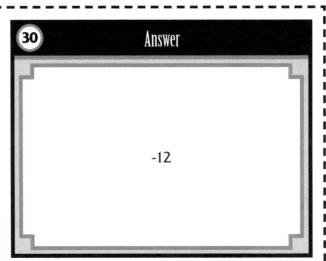

30 Answer

-12

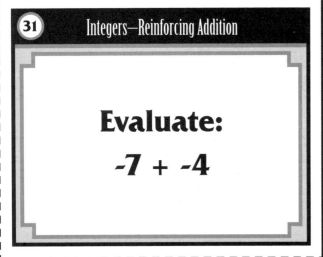

31 Integers—Reinforcing Addition

Evaluate:
-7 + -4

31 Answer

-11

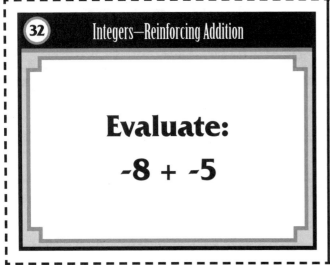

32 Integers—Reinforcing Addition

Evaluate:
-8 + -5

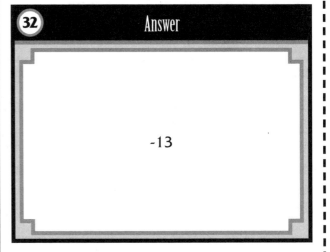

32 Answer

-13

Integers— Reinforcing Subtraction

Integers—Reinforcing Subtraction Quiz-Quiz-Trade cards reinforce students' conceptual understanding of subtracting positive and negative integers.

Sample Cards

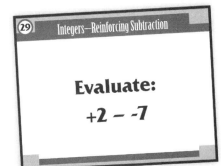

Integers—Reinforcing Subtraction

Directions: Subtract the given integers.

Integers—Reinforcing
Subtraction

Card Set Label

When it's time to store this set, place this card label at the top of the set so that it's easy to identify for the next use.

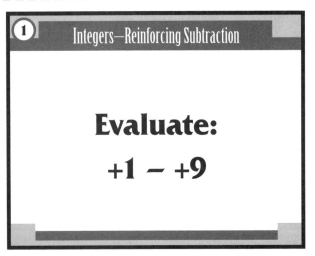

1 | Integers—Reinforcing Subtraction

Evaluate:
+1 − +9

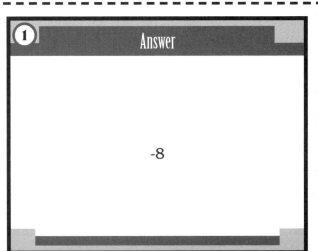

1 | Answer

-8

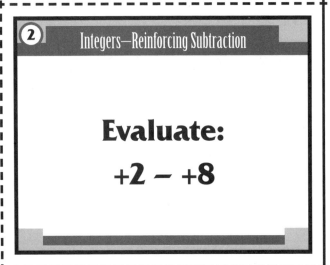

2 | Integers—Reinforcing Subtraction

Evaluate:
+2 − +8

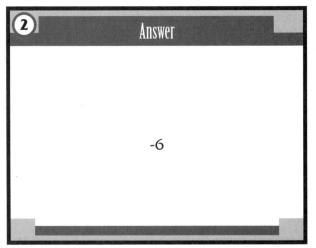

2 | Answer

-6

Directions: Subtract the given integers.

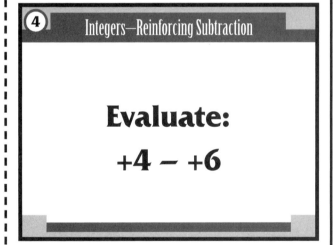

Integers—Reinforcing Subtraction

Evaluate:
+3 − +7

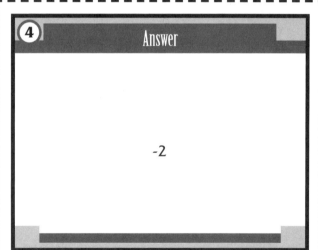

Answer

-4

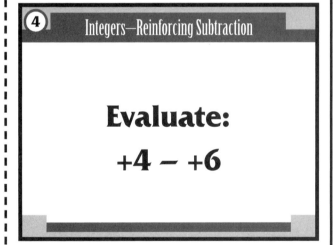

Integers—Reinforcing Subtraction

Evaluate:
+4 − +6

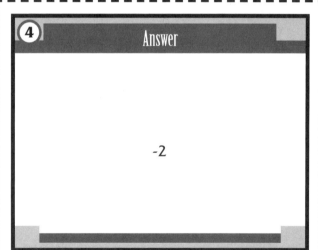

Answer

-2

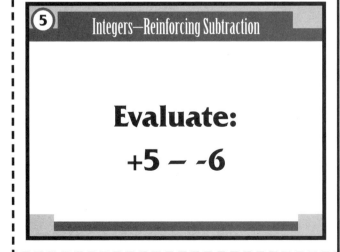

Integers—Reinforcing Subtraction

Evaluate:
+5 − -6

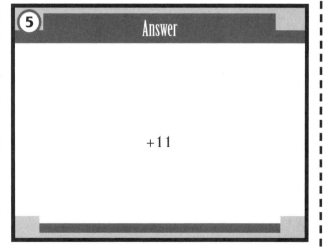

Answer

+11

Integers—Reinforcing Subtraction

Directions: Subtract the given integers.

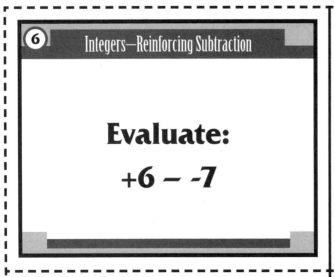

6 Integers—Reinforcing Subtraction

Evaluate:

+6 – -7

6 Answer

+13

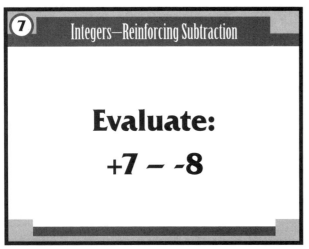

7 Integers—Reinforcing Subtraction

Evaluate:

+7 – -8

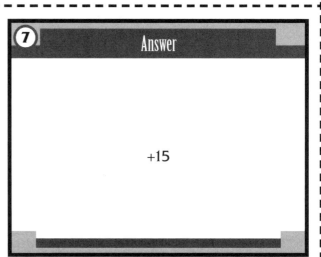

7 Answer

+15

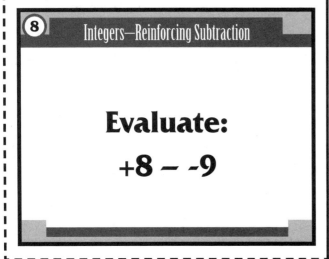

8 Integers—Reinforcing Subtraction

Evaluate:

+8 – -9

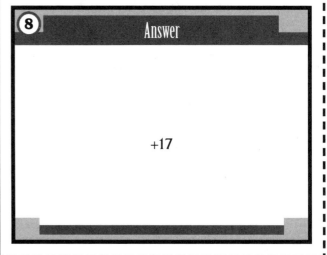

8 Answer

+17

Integers—Reinforcing Subtraction

Directions: Subtract the given integers.

9 Integers—Reinforcing Subtraction	**9** Answer
Evaluate: **+9 – -1**	+10
10 Integers—Reinforcing Subtraction	**10** Answer
Evaluate: **0 – -2**	+2
11 Integers—Reinforcing Subtraction	**11** Answer
Evaluate: **+1 – -3**	+4

Integers—Reinforcing Subtraction

Directions: Subtract the given integers.

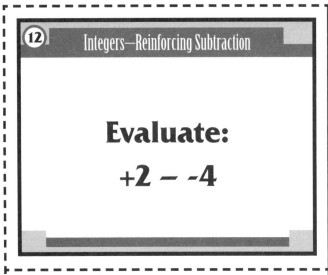

12 Integers—Reinforcing Subtraction

Evaluate:
+2 − -4

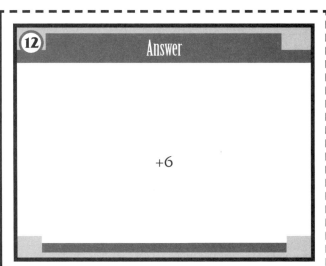

12 Answer

+6

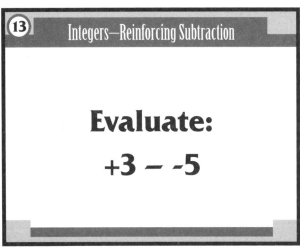

13 Integers—Reinforcing Subtraction

Evaluate:
+3 − -5

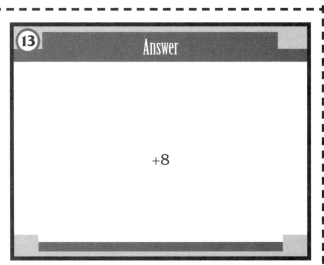

13 Answer

+8

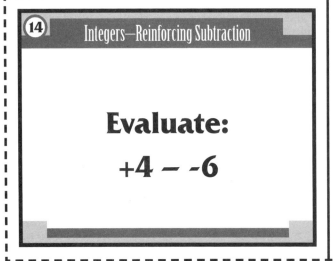

14 Integers—Reinforcing Subtraction

Evaluate:
+4 − -6

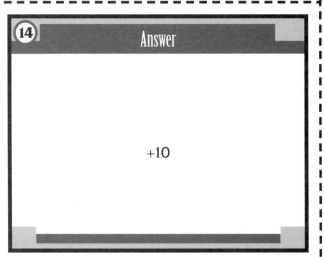

14 Answer

+10

Integers—Reinforcing Subtraction

Directions: Subtract the given integers.

15 Integers—Reinforcing Subtraction

Evaluate:
+5 – -7

15 Answer

+12

16 Integers—Reinforcing Subtraction

Evaluate:
+6 – -8

16 Answer

+14

17 Integers—Reinforcing Subtraction

Evaluate:
-1 – -9

17 Answer

+8

Integers—Reinforcing Subtraction

Directions: Subtract the given integers.

18 Integers—Reinforcing Subtraction **Evaluate:** **-2 – -8**	**18** Answer +6
19 Integers—Reinforcing Subtraction **Evaluate:** **-3 – -7**	**19** Answer +4
20 Integers—Reinforcing Subtraction **Evaluate:** **-4 – -6**	**20** Answer +2

Integers—Reinforcing Subtraction

Directions: Subtract the given integers.

21 Integers—Reinforcing Subtraction

Evaluate:
-5 – -5

21 Answer

0

22 Integers—Reinforcing Subtraction

Evaluate:
-6 – -4

22 Answer

-2

23 Integers—Reinforcing Subtraction

Evaluate:
-7 – -3

23 Answer

-4

Integers—Reinforcing Subtraction

Directions: Subtract the given integers.

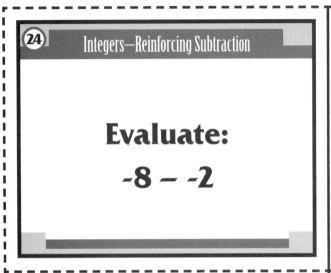

24 Integers—Reinforcing Subtraction

Evaluate:
-8 – -2

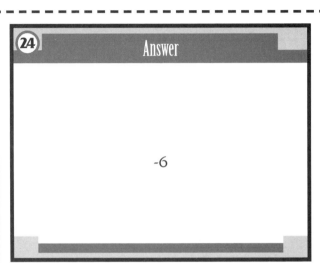

24 Answer

-6

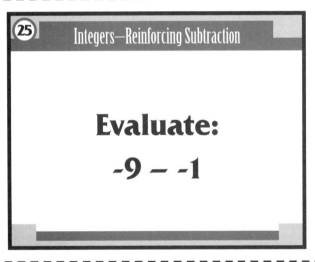

25 Integers—Reinforcing Subtraction

Evaluate:
-9 – -1

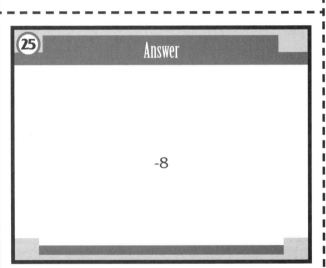

25 Answer

-8

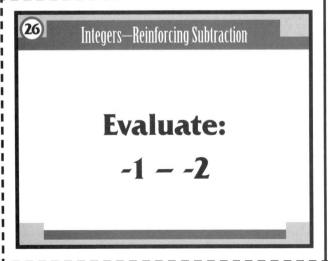

26 Integers—Reinforcing Subtraction

Evaluate:
-1 – -2

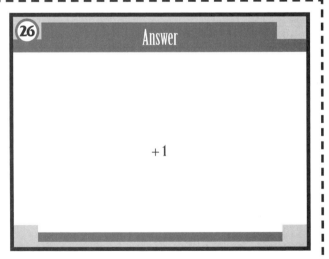

26 Answer

+1

Integers—Reinforcing Subtraction

Directions: Subtract the given integers.

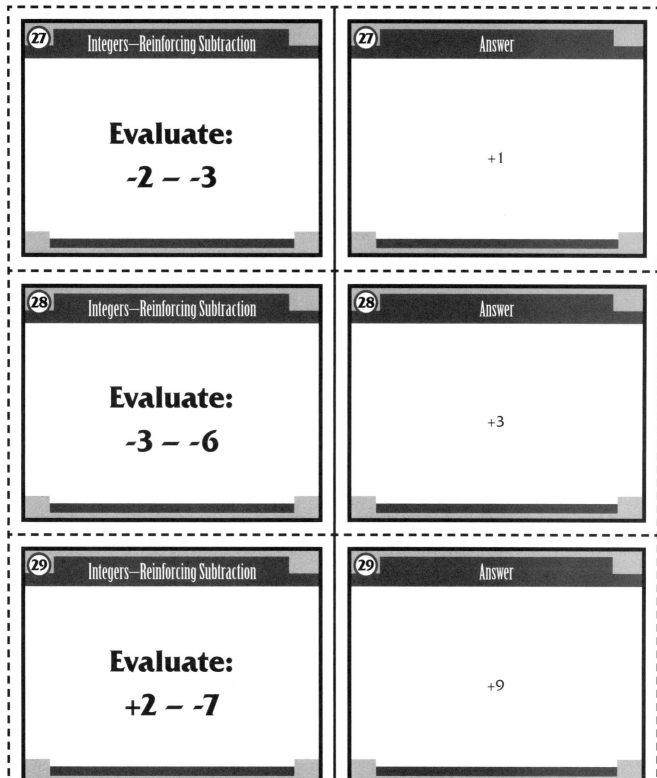

27 Integers—Reinforcing Subtraction

Evaluate:
-2 – -3

27 Answer

+1

28 Integers—Reinforcing Subtraction

Evaluate:
-3 – -6

28 Answer

+3

29 Integers—Reinforcing Subtraction

Evaluate:
+2 – -7

29 Answer

+9

Integers—Reinforcing Subtraction

Directions: Subtract the given integers.

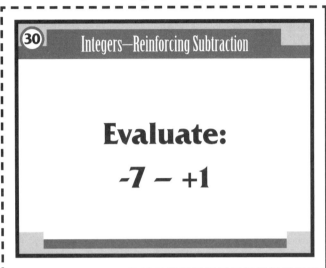

30 Integers—Reinforcing Subtraction

Evaluate:
-7 – +1

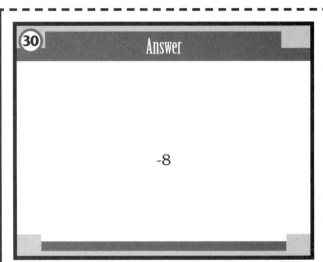

30 Answer

-8

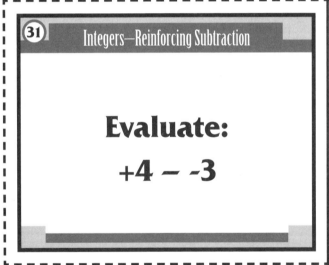

31 Integers—Reinforcing Subtraction

Evaluate:
+4 – -3

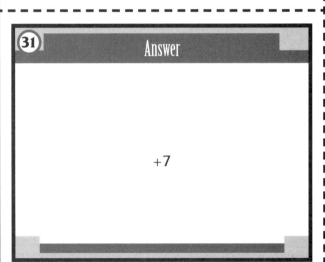

31 Answer

+7

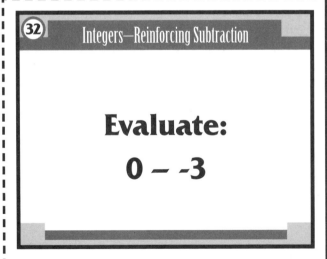

32 Integers—Reinforcing Subtraction

Evaluate:
0 – -3

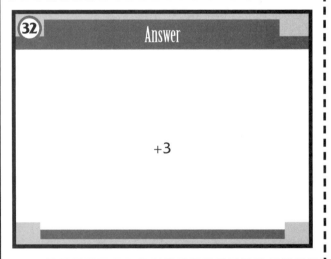

32 Answer

+3

Order of Operations

Order of Operations Quiz-Quiz-Trade cards reinforce students' conceptual understanding of determining the appropriate order in which to perform operations (adding, subtracting, multiplying, and dividing). The acronym PEMDAS is used, with the understanding that exponents are not part of the Level 2 curriculum.

Sample Cards

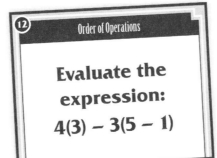

(12) Order of Operations

Evaluate the expression:
$4(3) - 3(5 - 1)$

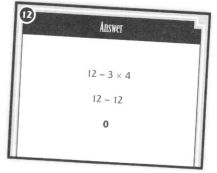

(12) Answer

$12 - 3 \times 4$

$12 - 12$

0

Order of Operations

Directions: Evaluate the given expression correctly using the order of operations.

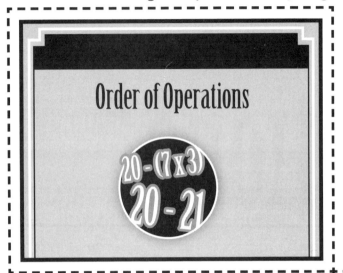

Order of Operations

Card Set Label

When it's time to store this set, place this card label at the top of the set so that it's easy to identify for the next use.

---

1 Order of Operations

What does the acronym PEMDAS stand for?

1 Answer

Parentheses
Exponents
Multiplication
Division
Addition
Subtraction

---

2 Order of Operations

What is the last thing to resolve when solving multi-step equations or expressions?

2 Answer

addition and/or subtraction

Order of Operations

Directions: Evaluate the given expression correctly using the order of operations.

3 Order of Operations	**3** Answer
Evaluate the expression: $20 \div (3 + 2) - 5$	$20 \div 5 - 5$ $4 - 5$ **-1**
4 Order of Operations	**4** Answer
Evaluate the expression: $100 - 7 \times 7 - 1$	$100 - 49 - 1$ **50**
5 Order of Operations	**5** Answer
Evaluate the expression: $4 \times 7 - (9 - 5) \div 2$	$28 - 4 \div 2$ $28 - 2$ **26**

Order of Operations

Directions: Evaluate the given expression correctly using the order of operations.

6 Order of Operations

Evaluate the expression:
$20 - (7 \times 3)$

6 Answer

$20 - 21$

-1

7 Order of Operations

Evaluate the expression:
$8 - 9 \div 3 - 5$

7 Answer

$8 - 3 - 5$

0

8 Order of Operations

Evaluate the expression:
$6(7 - 3) \div 8 - 4$

8 Answer

$6 \times 4 \div 8 - 4$

$3 - 4$

-1

Quiz-Quiz-Trade: Middle School Math
Kagan Publishing • 800.933.2667 • www.KaganOnline.com

Order of Operations

$\dfrac{20 - (7 \times 3)}{20 - 21}$

Directions: Evaluate the given expression correctly using the order of operations.

⑨ Order of Operations

Evaluate the expression:
$$21 - 4 \times 7 + 8$$

⑨ Answer

$21 - 28 + 8$

1

⑩ Order of Operations

Evaluate the expression:
$$4 + 4(7 - 3)$$

⑩ Answer

$4 + 4 \times 4$

$4 + 16$

20

⑪ Order of Operations

Evaluate the expression:
$$32 - 3(2 + 7)$$

⑪ Answer

$32 - 3(9)$

$32 - 27$

5

Order of Operations

Directions: Evaluate the given expression correctly using the order of operations.

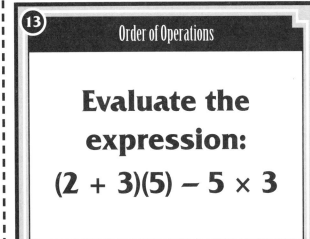

⑫ Order of Operations

Evaluate the expression: 4(3) − 3(5 − 1)

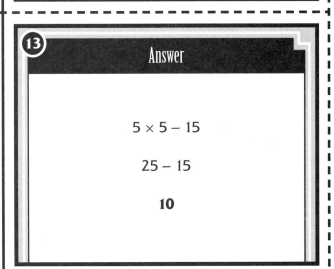

⑫ Answer

12 − 3 × 4

12 − 12

0

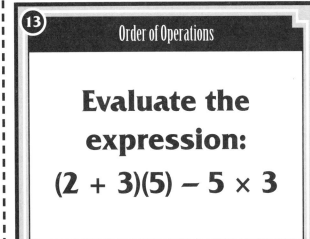

⑬ Order of Operations

Evaluate the expression: (2 + 3)(5) − 5 × 3

⑬ Answer

5 × 5 − 15

25 − 15

10

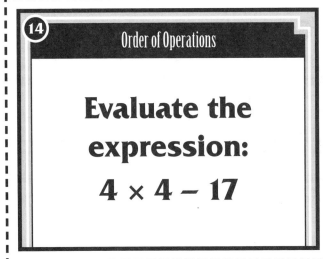

⑭ Order of Operations

Evaluate the expression: 4 × 4 − 17

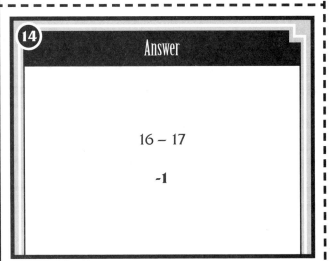

⑭ Answer

16 − 17

-1

Order of Operations

Directions: Evaluate the given expression correctly using the order of operations.

---

15 Order of Operations

Evaluate the expression:
3(2 − -2)

15 Answer

3×4

12

---

16 Order of Operations

Evaluate the expression:
3 + 5(6) − 4 × 7

16 Answer

$3 + 30 - 28$

5

---

17 Order of Operations

Evaluate the expression:
5 − 4(7 − 3) − -1

17 Answer

$5 - 4 \times 4 + 1$

$5 - 16 + 1$

-10

Order of Operations

Directions: Evaluate the given expression correctly using the order of operations.

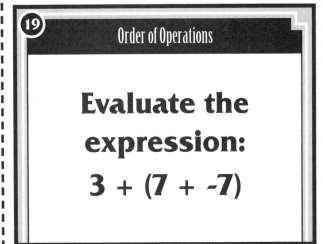

18 Order of Operations

Evaluate the expression:
$$3 \times 9 - 9 \div 3$$

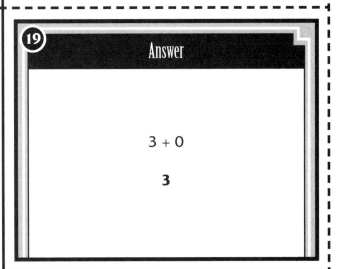

18 Answer

$27 - 3$

24

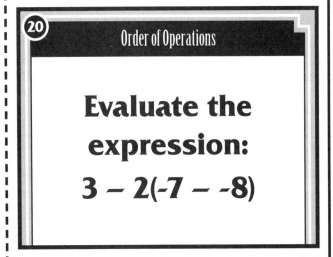

19 Order of Operations

Evaluate the expression:
$$3 + (7 + {-7})$$

19 Answer

$3 + 0$

3

20 Order of Operations

Evaluate the expression:
$$3 - 2({-7} - {-8})$$

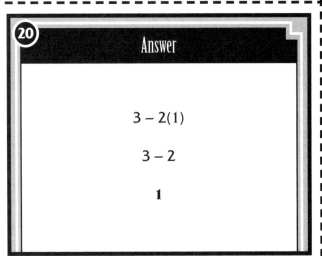

20 Answer

$3 - 2(1)$

$3 - 2$

1

Order of Operations

Directions: Evaluate the given expression correctly using the order of operations.

---

21 Order of Operations

Evaluate the expression:

16 − 4 × 4 − -5

---

21 Answer

16 − 16 + 5

5

---

22 Order of Operations

Evaluate the expression:

8(0) − 1(1)

---

22 Answer

0 − 1

-1

---

23 Order of Operations

Evaluate the expression:

(11 − -7) ÷ 3

---

23 Answer

18 ÷ 3

6

Order of Operations

Directions: Evaluate the given expression correctly using the order of operations.

24 Order of Operations

Evaluate the expression:
$17 - (11 - \text{-}8)$

24 Answer

$17 - 19$

-2

25 Order of Operations

Evaluate the expression:
$3(4 - 24 \div 6)$

25 Answer

$3(4 - 4)$

3×0

0

26 Order of Operations

Evaluate the expression:
$6 \times 3 \div 9 - 12 \div 4$

26 Answer

$2 - 3$

-1

Order of Operations

Directions: Evaluate the given expression correctly using the order of operations.

27 Order of Operations	**27** Answer
Evaluate the expression: $0(7 - 12 \div 3)$	0
28 Order of Operations	**28** Answer
Evaluate the expression: $15 - 3 \times 4 - \text{-}2$	$15 - 12 + 2$ 5
29 Order of Operations	**29** Answer
Evaluate the expression: $24 \div 3 - 3 \times 4$	$8 - 12$ -4

Order of Operations

Directions: Evaluate the given expression correctly using the order of operations.

---

30 | Order of Operations

Evaluate the expression:
21 ÷ 7 × 4 − -3

---

30 | Answer

12 + 3

15

---

31 | Order of Operations

Compare 3 × 8 ÷ 2 and 3 × (8 ÷ 2).

Are they the same? Explain.

---

31 | Answer

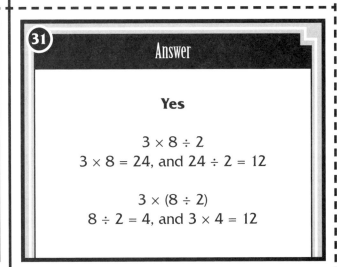

Yes

3 × 8 ÷ 2
3 × 8 = 24, and 24 ÷ 2 = 12

3 × (8 ÷ 2)
8 ÷ 2 = 4, and 3 × 4 = 12

---

32 | Order of Operations

Compare 24 ÷ 6 × 2 and 24 ÷ (6 × 2).

Are they the same? Explain.

---

32 | Answer

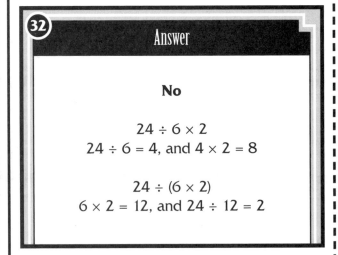

No

24 ÷ 6 × 2
24 ÷ 6 = 4, and 4 × 2 = 8

24 ÷ (6 × 2)
6 × 2 = 12, and 24 ÷ 12 = 2

Patterns & Relations

Patterns & Relations Quiz-Quiz-Trade cards reinforce students' conceptual understanding of all four quadrants of a coordinate grid; the horizontal and vertical axes; ordered pairs; the origin; how an input/output table, linear graph, and pattern rule are connected; and modeling expressions using algebra tiles.

Sample Cards

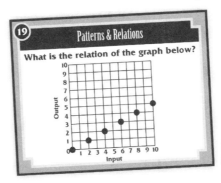

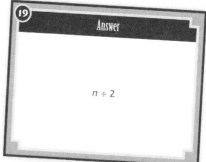

Patterns & Relations

Directions: Answer the question using your knowledge of patterns, relations, and the coordinate grid.

Card Set Label

When it's time to store this set, place this card label at the top of the set so that it's easy to identify for the next use.

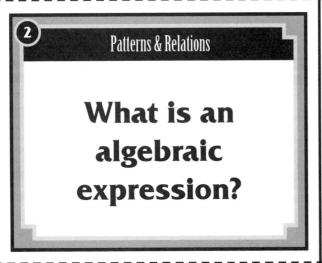

① Patterns & Relations

What is a variable?

① Answer

A variable is a letter or symbol representing a quantity that can vary.

Example: In the expression $5n - 3$, n is the variable.

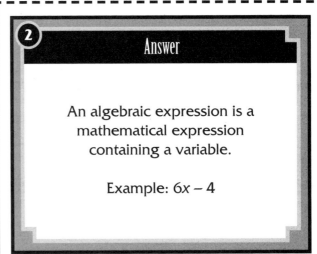

② Patterns & Relations

What is an algebraic expression?

② Answer

An algebraic expression is a mathematical expression containing a variable.

Example: $6x - 4$

Quiz-Quiz-Trade: Middle School Math
Kagan Publishing · 800.933.2667 · www.KaganOnline.com

Patterns & Relations

Directions: Answer the question using your knowledge of patterns, relations, and the coordinate grid.

---

3   Patterns & Relations

What is a numerical coefficient?

---

3   Answer

A numerical coefficient is the number by which a variable is multiplied.

Example: In the expression $4x + 3$, 4 is the numerical coefficient.

---

4   Patterns & Relations

What is a constant term?

---

4   Answer

A constant term is the number in an expression or equation that does not change.

Example: In the expression $4x + 3$, 3 is the constant term.

---

5   Patterns & Relations

What is an expression?

---

5   Answer

An expression is a mathematical phrase made up of numbers and/or variables connected by operations. It does not include an equals sign.

Example: $3x - 2$

Patterns & Relations

Directions: Answer the question using your knowledge of patterns, relations, and the coordinate grid.

6 Patterns & Relations

What is a linear relation?

6 Answer

A linear relation is a relation whose points lie on a straight line.

Example: $y = 2x + 1$

7 Patterns & Relations

What is a unit tile?

7 Answer

A unit tile is a tile that represents +1 or -1. Yellow is a positive unit tile and red is a negative unit tile.

Example: Y R

8 Patterns & Relations

What is an *x* tile or a variable tile?

8 Answer

An *x* tile is a tile that represents a variable. Yellow is a positive *x* tile and red is a negative *x* tile.

Example: X

Patterns & Relations

Directions: Answer the question using your knowledge of patterns, relations, and the coordinate grid.

---

9 Patterns & Relations

What is a relation?

---

9 Answer

A linear relation is a set of input (x) values and output (y) values, usually represented in ordered pairs. Example: $y = 3x - 1$. The ordered pairs are (1, 2), (3, 8) and (5, 14) as taken from the table of values.

Example:

x	y
1	2
3	8
5	14

---

10 Patterns & Relations

Define algebra tiles.

---

10 Answer

Algebra tiles are a collective term for unit tiles and variable tiles.

---

11 Patterns & Relations

Define isolating the variable.

---

11 Answer

Isolating the variable is a step used to solve an algebraic equation. It may be necessary to rearrange terms, collect like terms, and use one or more inverse operations to get the variable by itself (solve the equation).

Patterns & Relations

Directions: Answer the question using your knowledge of patterns, relations, and the coordinate grid.

12 Patterns & Relations

The pattern rule is
multiply by 2, then add 3.
Is the following table correct?

Input	Output
1	5
2	6
3	9
4	11

12 Answer

No

When the input is 2,
the output should be 7.

13 Patterns & Relations

The pattern rule is
multiply by 3, then subtract 1.
Is the following table correct?

Input	Output
1	2
2	5
3	8
4	11

13 Answer

Yes

14 Patterns & Relations

The pattern rule is
multiply by 2, then add 5.
Is the following table correct?

Input	Output
1	7
2	9
3	12
4	13

14 Answer

No

When the input is 3,
the output should be 11.

Patterns & Relations

Directions: Answer the question using your knowledge of patterns, relations, and the coordinate grid.

15 Patterns & Relations

What is the relation for:

Input	Output
1	1
2	5
3	9
4	13
5	17
6	21

15 Answer

$$4n - 3$$

16 Patterns & Relations

Determine the relation and find the missing output for:

Input	Output
3	10
4	13
5	16
6	
7	

16 Answer

$$3n + 1$$

Input	Output
6	**19**
7	**22**

17 Patterns & Relations

Determine the relation and find the missing output for:

Input	Output
2	4
3	7
4	10
5	
6	

17 Answer

$$3n - 2$$

Input	Output
5	**13**
6	**16**

Patterns & Relations

Directions: Answer the question using your knowledge of patterns, relations, and the coordinate grid.

18 Patterns & Relations

Determine the relation and find the missing output for:

Input	Output
1	1
3	5
5	9
7	
9	

18 Answer

$2n - 1$

Input	Output
7	**13**
9	**17**

19 Patterns & Relations

What is the relation of the graph below?

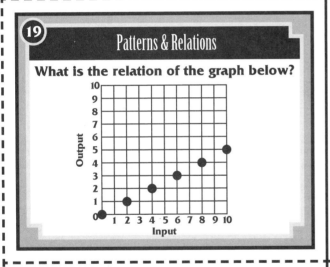

19 Answer

$n \div 2$

20 Patterns & Relations

What is the relation of the graph below?

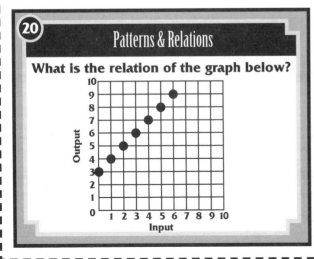

20 Answer

$n + 3$

Patterns & Relations

Directions: Answer the question using your knowledge of patterns, relations, and the coordinate grid.

21 Patterns & Relations

What is the relation of the graph below?

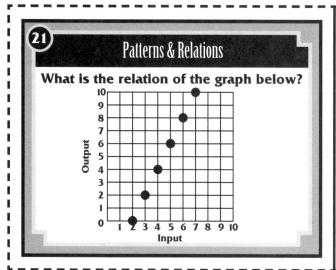

21 Answer

$2n - 4$

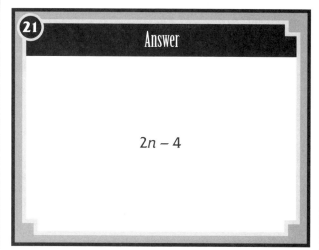

22 Patterns & Relations

What is the relation of the graph below?

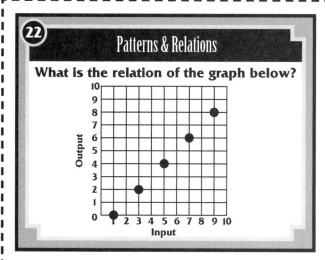

22 Answer

$n - 1$

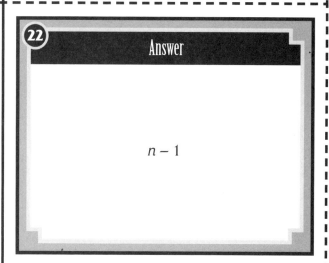

23 Patterns & Relations

Write a relation for the term:

Term #	1	2	3	4	5
Term	6	12	18	24	30

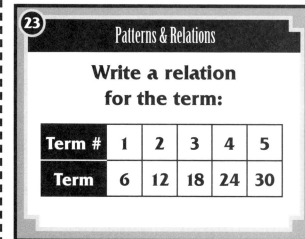

23 Answer

$6n$

Patterns & Relations

Directions: Answer the question using your knowledge of patterns, relations, and the coordinate grid.

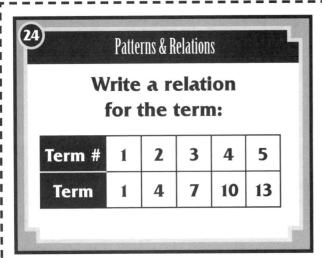

24

Patterns & Relations

Write a relation for the term:

Term #	1	2	3	4	5
Term	1	4	7	10	13

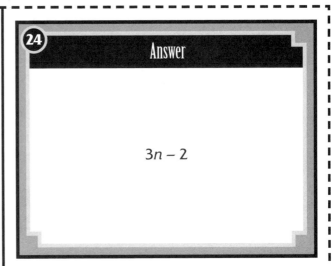

24 Answer

$3n - 2$

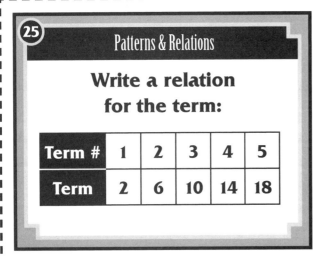

25

Patterns & Relations

Write a relation for the term:

Term #	1	2	3	4	5
Term	2	6	10	14	18

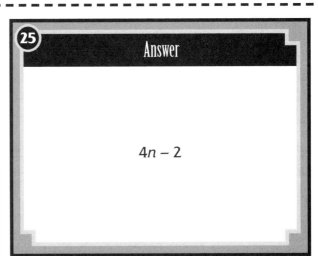

25 Answer

$4n - 2$

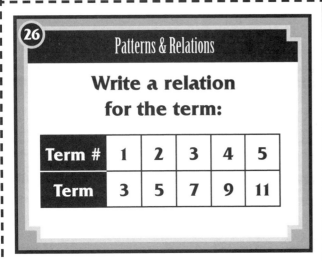

26

Patterns & Relations

Write a relation for the term:

Term #	1	2	3	4	5
Term	3	5	7	9	11

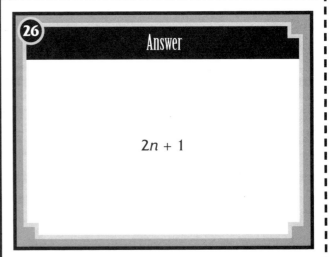

26 Answer

$2n + 1$

Patterns & Relations

Directions: Answer the question using your knowledge of patterns, relations, and the coordinate grid.

27 — Patterns & Relations

Write an expression for: 2 more than a number

27 — Answer

$$n + 2$$

28 — Patterns & Relations

Write an expression for: a number multiplied by 3

28 — Answer

$$3n$$

29 — Patterns & Relations

Write an expression for: 4 less than a number

29 — Answer

$$n - 4$$

Patterns & Relations

Directions: Answer the question using your knowledge of patterns, relations, and the coordinate grid.

30 Patterns & Relations

Write an expression for: quadruple a number and add 5

30 Answer

$$4n + 5$$

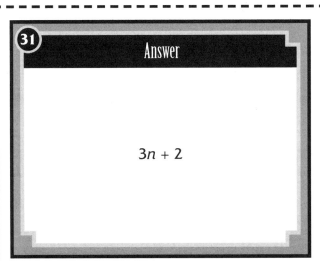

31 Patterns & Relations

Write an expression for: triple a number and add 2

31 Answer

$$3n + 2$$

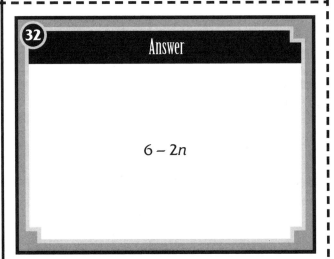

32 Patterns & Relations

Write an expression for: a number is doubled and subtracted from 6

32 Answer

$$6 - 2n$$

Transformations

Transformations Quiz-Quiz-Trade cards reinforce students' conceptual understanding of all four quadrants of a coordinate grid, the horizontal and vertical axes, ordered pairs, the origin, rotations, translations, and reflections.

Sample Cards

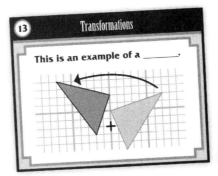

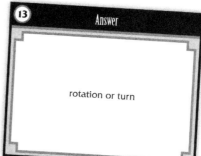

Transformations

Directions: Answer each question using your knowledge of transformations.

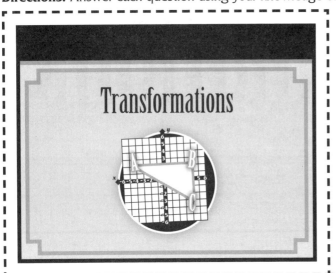

Transformations

1 Transformations

What is a transformation?

1 Answer

A transformation refers to the movement of objects in the coordinate plane. It may be a translation (slide), a reflection (flip), or a rotation (turn).

2 Transformations

What is the origin?

2 Answer

The origin is the point where the x-axis and y-axis intersect (0, 0).

Transformations

Directions: Answer each question using your knowledge of transformations.

3 Transformations

x-axis

3 Answer

The *x*-axis is the horizontal number line on a coordinate grid or Cartesian plane.

4 Transformations

y-axis

4 Answer

The *y*-axis is the vertical number line on a coordinate grid or Cartesian plane.

5 Transformations

What is a rotation?

5 Answer

A rotation is a transformation in which a shape is turned or rotated about a fixed point.

Transformations

Directions: Answer each question using your knowledge of transformations.

---

6 Transformations

What is a translation?

---

6 Answer

A translation is a transformation that moves a point or a shape in a straight line to another position on the same flat surface.

---

7 Transformations

What is a reflection?

---

7 Answer

A reflection is a transformation that is illustrated by a shape and its image in a mirror line.

---

8 Transformations

How is A' read?

---

8 Answer

"A prime"

Transformations

Directions: Answer each question using your knowledge of transformations.

9 Transformations **The coordinates of point *A* are (-3, 4). Which quadrant is point *A* in?**	**9** Answer Quadrant II
10 Transformations **The coordinates of point *Z* are (4, -1). Which quadrant is point *Z* in?**	**10** Answer Quadrant IV
11 Transformations **The coordinates of point *B* are (-5, -4). Which quadrant is point *B* in?**	**11** Answer Quadrant III

Transformations

Directions: Answer each question using your knowledge of transformations.

12 Transformations	12 Answer

The coordinates of point C are (3, 5). Which quadrant is point C in?

Quadrant I

13 Transformations	13 Answer

This is an example of a _____.

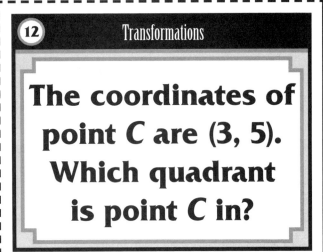

rotation or turn

14 Transformations	14 Answer

This is an example of a _____.

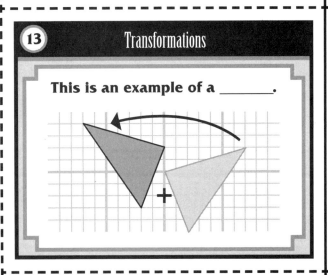

reflection or flip

Transformations

Directions: Answer each question using your knowledge of transformations.

---

15 | Transformations

This is an example of a _____.

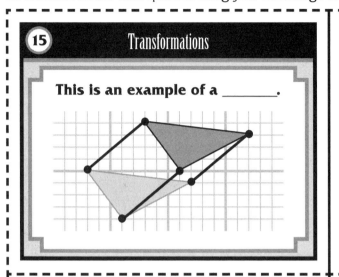

15 | Answer

translation or slide

---

16 | Transformations

If you reflect across the *y*-axis, what will *A*′ be?

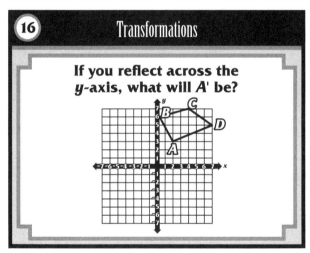

16 | Answer

(-2, 3)

---

17 | Transformations

If you reflect across the *x*-axis, what will *A*′ be?

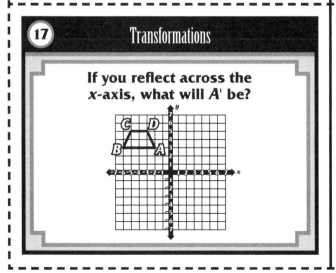

17 | Answer

(-2, -3)

Quiz-Quiz-Trade: Middle School Math

Kagan Publishing · 800.933.2667 · www.KaganOnline.com

199

Transformations

Directions: Answer each question using your knowledge of transformations.

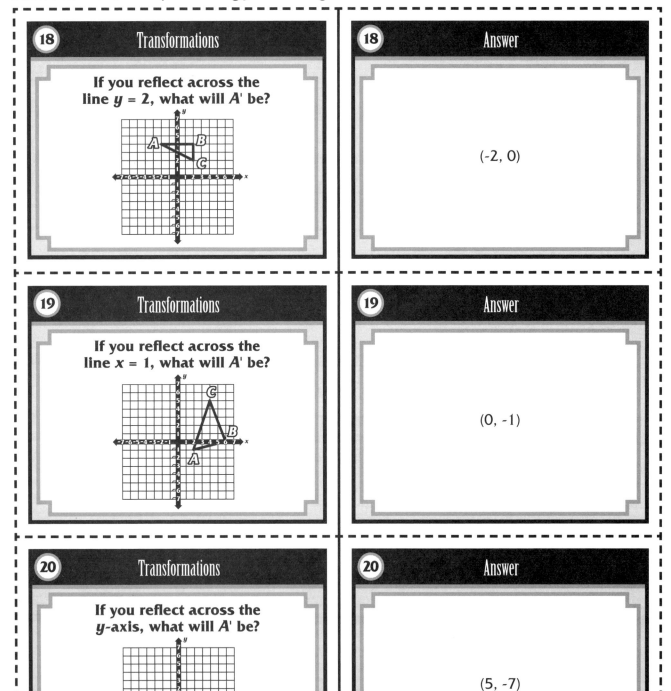

18 Transformations

If you reflect across the line $y = 2$, what will A' be?

18 Answer

(-2, 0)

19 Transformations

If you reflect across the line $x = 1$, what will A' be?

19 Answer

(0, -1)

20 Transformations

If you reflect across the y-axis, what will A' be?

20 Answer

(5, -7)

Transformations

Directions: Answer each question using your knowledge of transformations.

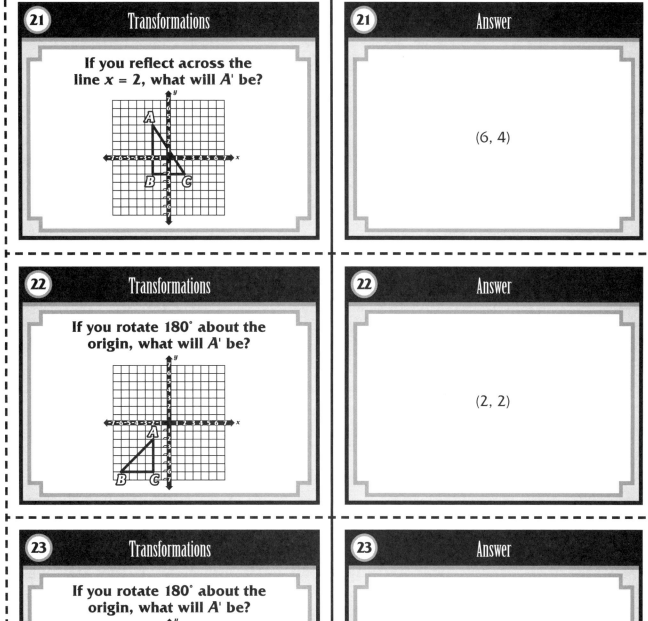

21 Transformations

If you reflect across the line *x* = 2, what will *A'* be?

21 Answer

(6, 4)

22 Transformations

If you rotate 180˚ about the origin, what will *A'* be?

22 Answer

(2, 2)

23 Transformations

If you rotate 180˚ about the origin, what will *A'* be?

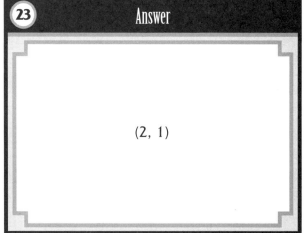

23 Answer

(2, 1)

Transformations

Directions: Answer each question using your knowledge of transformations.

24 Transformations

If you rotate 90° clockwise about the origin, what will *A*' be?

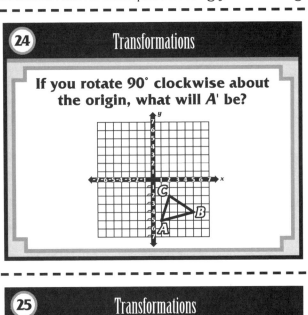

24 Answer

(-5, -1)

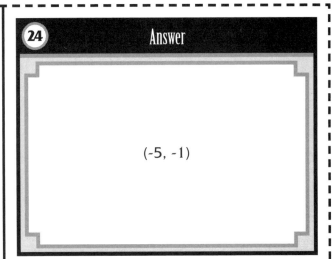

25 Transformations

If you rotate 180° about the origin, what will *A*' be?

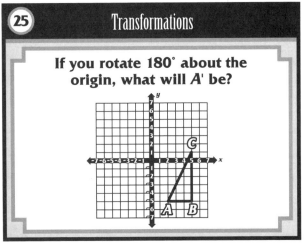

25 Answer

(-2, 5)

26 Transformations

If you rotate 90° counterclockwise about the origin, what will *A*' be?

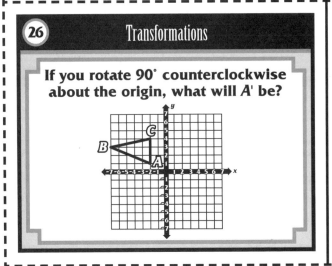

26 Answer

(-1, -2)

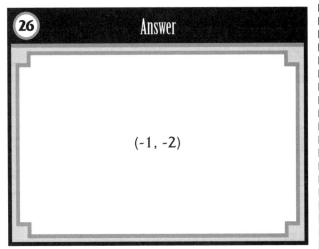

Quiz-Quiz-Trade: Middle School Math
Kagan Publishing · 800.933.2667 · www.KaganOnline.com

Transformations

Directions: Answer each question using your knowledge of transformations.

---

27 | Transformations

If you translate 7 units left and 4 units up, what will *A'* be?

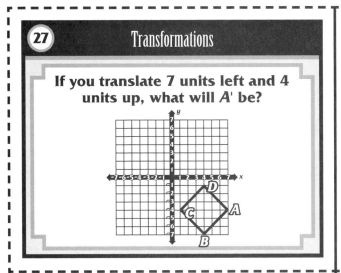

27 | Answer

(0, 0)

---

28 | Transformations

If you translate 5 units right and 4 units down, what will *A'* be?

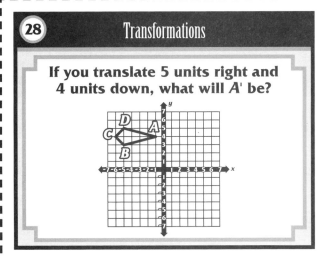

28 | Answer

(4, 0)

---

29 | Transformations

If you translate 2 units right and 4 units up, what will *A'* be?

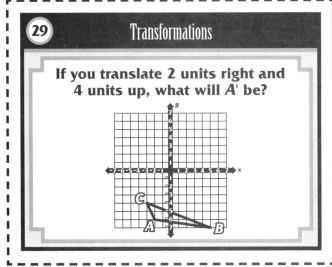

29 | Answer

(0, -2)

Transformations

Directions: Answer each question using your knowledge of transformations.

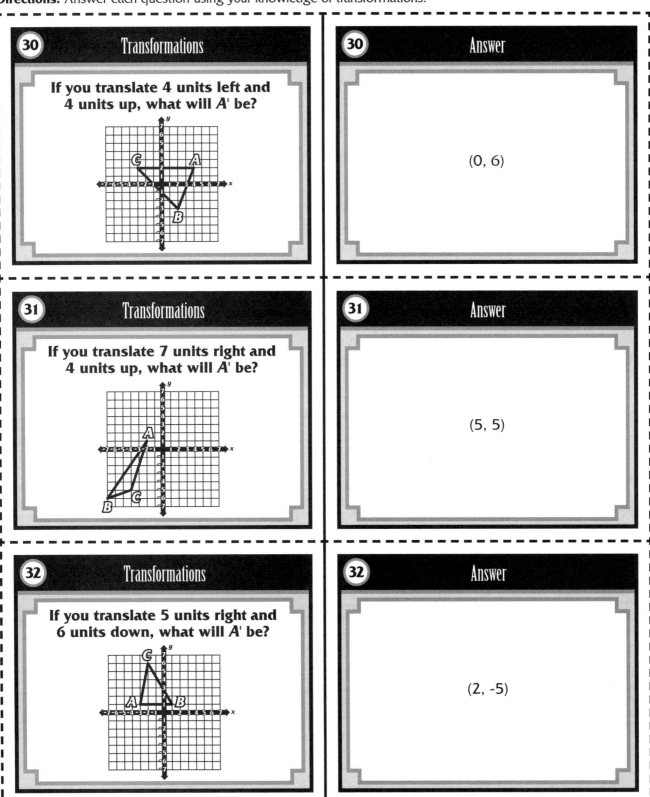

30 Transformations

If you translate 4 units left and 4 units up, what will A' be?

30 Answer

(0, 6)

31 Transformations

If you translate 7 units right and 4 units up, what will A' be?

31 Answer

(5, 5)

32 Transformations

If you translate 5 units right and 6 units down, what will A' be?

32 Answer

(2, -5)

Quiz-Quiz-Trade: Middle School Math
Kagan Publishing • 800.933.2667 • www.KaganOnline.com